THE
CREATIVITY
BOOK

it's a God thing!

Other Books Available

The Lily Series

    Here's Lily!
    Lily Robbins, M.D. (Medical Dabbler)
    Lily and the Creep
    Lily's Ultimate Party
    Ask Lily
    Lily the Rebel
    Lights, Action, Lily!
    Lily Rules!
    Rough & Rugged Lily
    Lily Speaks!
    Horse Crazy Lily
    Lily's Church Camp Adventure
    Lily's Passport to Paris
    Lily's in London?!

Nonfiction

    The Beauty Book
    The Body Book
    The Buddy Book
    The Best Bash Book
    The Blurry Rules Book
    The It's MY Life Book
    The Creativity Book
    The Uniquely Me Book
    The Year 'Round Holiday Book
    The Values & Virtues Book
    The Fun-Finder Book
    The Walk-the-Walk Book
    Dear Diary
    Girlz Want to Know
    NIV Young Women of Faith Bible
    Hey! This Is Me Journal
    Take It from Me

THE CREATIVITY BOOK

it's a God thing!

Written by Nancy Rue
Illustrated by Lyn Boyer

Zonderkidz

Zonder**kidz**®

The children's group of Zondervan

www.zonderkidz.com

The Creativity Book
Copyright © 2002 by Young Women of Faith

Requests for information should be addressed to:

Zonderkidz, *Grand Rapids, Michigan 49530*

ISBN: 0–310–70247-X

Published in association with the literary agency of Alive Communications, Inc., 7680 Goddard Street, Suite 200, Colorado Springs, CO 80920.

Editor: Barbara J. Scott
Interior design: Michelle Lenger
Art Direction: Michelle Lenger
Printed in the United States of America

05 06 07 / ❖ DC / 5 4 3 2

Contents

Who Said You Weren't Creative?

**In the beginning God created
the heavens and the earth.**
Genesis 1:1

Please do Not Disturb Daydreaming In Progress...

Think back to the last time you heard a teacher say, "I want you to be creative on this assignment."

Did you, like **Lily**, have more ideas than you could ever do and, in your head, they kept raising their hands and repeating, *Pick me! Pick me!*

Or, like **Reni**, did you think to yourself, *Well, I play an instrument, and I can draw okay. I guess I could do one of those.*

Were you more like **Kresha**, thinking, *I can't make anything but cookies—and faces at my little brother. Are those creative?*

Maybe **Suzy**'s reaction was more like yours: *What if I create something and my teacher doesn't like it? What if I fail?*

Or did you fall into **Zooey**'s camp: *I'm not creative! I can't do anything like that! It's a waste of time to try! I'm a loser!*

If asked to be creative, would you respond like any of our Girlz did? If so, this book is for you. Even if you have some other reason for doubting that you have a creative side, keep reading. *Everybody*—that's each and every person ever born—is creative in some way. It comes with the "you" package.

Every person—including you—has the ability to make art in some way. That just means that you take an idea from your mind and make it into something that can be enjoyed, even if it's just by you and you alone. There are tons of ways it can be done:

Baking a cake	Decorating a room	Styling hair
Planning a party	Making babies laugh	Painting faces
Planting a garden	Making up a game	Creating a costume
Writing a letter	Making a birthday card	Wrapping a present
Making a sandwich	Writing new words to a song	Making up a dance
Cheering up a friend	Reading a book out loud	Writing in a diary

Decorating cookies   Keeping a scrapbook   Painting your toenails

Playing with a soccer ball Displaying a collection Singing in the shower

Making art isn't the painting, the toothpick structure, or the short story you end up with. It's the *process* of getting from an idea to a finished product—and it's a process that makes living much more fun. Just doing it can make you feel rich inside. The best news is—*anyone* can do it. We know it, of course, because—well—God says so!

HOW IS THIS A God Thing?

Probably the very first Bible story you ever learned was the story of creation (you know, the one where God created the heavens and the earth). Can you imagine what a blast that must have been for God? He got to decide what colors roses were going to be and come up with about a bajillion varieties of seashells (for your collecting pleasure!). Not to mention his sense of humor. When was the last time you took a good look at a rhinoceros?

Then, of course, there's you and all the other people he created—each one unique. You don't get more creative than that! Now think about the one thing that sets us humans apart from the rest of God's creation. "So God created man (humans) in his own image." And just to make sure we get it, he goes on to add, "in the image of God he created him" (Genesis 1:27).

What that means is that God made us to be like him—in a human form, of course. And just like him, we were born to create.

What that *doesn't* mean is that we can all:

- Draw cartoons like Charles Schultz.
- Write music like Stephen Curtis Chapman.
- Make up stories like those cool people who write *Adventures in Odyssey.*

Not everybody was born to be a *professional* artist, musician, or writer, but we can all:

- Experiment with our little creative sparks and feel God when we do it.
- Let God create through us in even small ways.
- Use our own special creativity as a way to thank God for all the creative things he does for us.

So when, like Lily, you get excited about creating some project, that's probably God saying, "You go, girl!"

When, like Reni, you aren't quite sure if playing the flute or doodling with paper and markers is creative, God's probably saying, "You're on the right track. Don't stop!"

When, like Kresha, you don't think putting your little brother in stitches with your hilarious faces is creative, God's probably saying, "Oh, Honey, yes! You've got *me* rolling on the floor of heaven!"

When, like Suzy, you're afraid you might fail, God's probably saying, "This is no time for fear, my love. Just have fun with this and see what happens."

And when, like Zooey, you feel about as creative as a dial tone, God is definitely saying, "You're wrong, my precious. I didn't create any dial tones."

We were all born to enjoy the process of making, creating, imagining, and concocting. God wants it that way. We just have to remember a couple of things. Let's call them the *creative cautions*:

- Once you get going on some creative project and everybody's saying, "Wow! That's cool!" it's tempting to start thinking, *I'm great! I'm terrific! I'm amazing!* Creating is way fun, but it's a gift from God. When somebody says, "Wow! That's cool!" the thing to think is, *Yeah—isn't God the best?*

- Sometimes when you're really cooking on something creative, you might find yourself thinking, *I'm better at this than she is. Come to think of it, I'm better at this than most people I know. Matter of fact—I'm the best!* That's about the time God shakes his head and says, "No, darlin'—this isn't about competition. Don't go there."

- At times when you've finished doing something creative and you're happy with it, you may think, *That's the best I can do. I've reached my limit.* Nope. There is *no* limit to how much God wants to give us and how much he wants to help us with our creative side.

- There may even be times when you're dreaming about doing great creative things and then you think, *Is this really what God wants me to do? Or am I just coming up with my own ideas because I want to be, like, famous or something?* There's always that possibility—but how will you know unless you turn those creative sparks into lights and see where they lead? Creativity isn't automatically anti-God. Not at all! But we think, *I should be doing something useful. I should be doing something to help people. I should be reading the Bible.* Creativity is about God, and it's one of the many things he has for us to do—right along with being useful, helpful, and biblical. Doing something creative is no more a guilty pleasure than eating a pizza covered with pepperoni.

✓ CHECK Yourself OUT

Now that you know that everybody—including you—is creative, let's find out what *kind* of creator you are. Not *how* creative you are—more than your sister, less than your best friend, that kind of thing—but *where* you shine. It's quiz time!

Before you sit down with your pencil (or maybe a purple gel pen or a big crayon in your favorite color?), find yourself a quiet, comfortable spot (on your bed surrounded by stuffed animals, up in a tree in your backyard, behind the couch in the family room with a glass of chocolate milk). Then go for it.

In each list below, put a check or a star (or whatever other creative mark you want to use) next to each activity you think would be fun to try. Pretend money, time, and permission from your parents and all those other limits in your life don't count. (They do, of course, but not while you're taking this quiz!) You don't have to already know how to do any of the things you check off—they just have to sound like fun to you.

_____ Planning a theme party (outer space, Hollywood, beach, St. Patrick's Day, that kind of thing)

_____ Putting together a hike for a bunch of your friends, complete with picnic lunch, special hiking hats, and songs to sing along the way

_____ Devising a hilarious scavenger hunt

_____ Having a theme movie night (maybe everybody watches *The Prince of Egypt* dressed like Egyptians or Hebrew slaves; you play "Does the Movie Match the Bible"; you all eat Passover food)

_____ Going all out for a sports event—like having a tailgate party before your brother's Little League game, wearing the team colors, making up a cheer to do from the stands

_____ Wearing a different style of outfit every day for a week (cowgirl one day, feminine and romantic the next, '70s flower child the next, etc.) with hairdo to match

_____ Putting together a scrapbook of all your friends and the stuff you've done together

_____ Redecorating your bedroom

_____ Making a different journal (with decorated cover, of course) for each different part of your life (one for your God experiences, one about friends, one about things you like in nature, one to complain in, etc.)

_____ Experimenting in the kitchen until you come up with perfect nachos

_____ Making a tribute to each member of your family—maybe by painting each person's portrait or writing a poem about each one or making up a song with a verse for each person

_____ Being part of a theatrical production—either as the playwright, the set designer, the lighting designer, the costumer, the musical director, the dance choreographer, an actor, or the director

_____ Going to an arts camp where you can learn about and play with music, visual arts (like painting, sculpture, drawing), acting, dance, writing—or any combination of those

_____ Helping to put together a creative worship service, using any or all of your musical, visual arts, acting, dancing, and writing talent

_____ Going on a trip to a foreign country where you would learn about that culture's music, visual arts, acting, dance, literature—some combination of those or even all of them

Let's find out where you shine. Count how many items you chose in each list and write the numbers below:

List 1 _____

List 2 _____

List 3 _____

If your *highest* number is in List 1, you shine most brightly in *creative activities*. You love—or would love—to plan unique parties and outings, and dream up cool ways to bring people together to do things besides sitting around playing video games and watching TV. You may never have thought about doing things like those on the list but noticed yourself getting jazzed when you read them. That means you're a "creative activities" person. If you pay attention to that part of yourself—which was put there by God—you're going to live a rich life, full of adventure and love and meaningful stuff done for God's glory. Pretty exciting, huh?

If your *highest* number is in List 2, you shine most brightly in *personal creativity*. You love—or would love—to design, make, dream up things that are fun for a person to do alone. Maybe you love clothes, cooking, decorating, and memorabilia (things like scrapbooks and photo albums and journals and autograph books). Perhaps you love to fix your friends' hair, explore your mother's jewelry box and get ideas for jewelry you'd like to make, or just snip pictures of things you like out of magazines. If you pay attention to that part of yourself—which was put there by God—not only are you going to be quietly happy with your lifestyle, but you're going to be a model for other people who may not be enjoying their lives so much. It's all about finding creative ways to express the "you" that God made you to be. Imagine how much fun that would be.

If your *highest* number is in List 3, you shine most brightly as an *artist*. You're interested in the things we usually think of when we say the word "art." These are areas like music, the visual arts (painting, drawing, sculpting, crafts, those kinds of things), dance, writing, and acting. You don't have to have tons of talent or be famous to enjoy those things. You just have to want to experience the fun of it—and you obviously do. Living an artist's life, even as an amateur dabbler who paints murals on the bathroom walls or makes up bedtime stories for her kids, can be a satisfying way to connect you with God and help you feel his pleasure in each small, artistic thing you do. What a great life that would be!

If you had almost the same *highest* number in two of the lists or high numbers in all of them, you've discovered more than one shining light in yourself. That doesn't mean you're more creative than other people—it just means you've already figured out that there are oodles of ways to express the "you" God made. It's possible for anybody to do that—or for people to simply shine WAY brightly in just one area. What matters is that you do the creative things you love to do. That pleases God.

If you had very few or no items marked, that does *not* mean you weren't created to be creative. Maybe your special thing just wasn't mentioned in the quiz. Or perhaps you should get somebody who knows you well to go through the quiz with you. That person may see things in you that you didn't even realize were there. In any case, keep reading! As you read, it's an almost certain guess that a light will go on in your head and you'll say, "Oh, yeah! I *am* creative after all!" That's why this book was written— to give you fun ways to get to know yourself better and discover that shining light of creativity God has placed in you. Get ready to be amazed!

Girlz WANT TO KNOW

You're sure to have some questions before we start. The Girlz definitely did. The answers to their questions could help to clear the way for you to explore your own creative self.

✿ *LILY: My mom says I'm a perfectionist about creative stuff, and it's true that I do like to get things right and fix things that turned out lame before I go any further on a project. I think I just have high standards. She says I'm missing out on the fun that way. Is she right?*

She is. (Don't you hate it when that happens?) You think you just want to make things perfect, but what's really happening is that you're not letting yourself keep going with a creative project. You get stuck fixing all the little details and pretty soon it isn't a creative project anymore. It's just doing something right. You can do math problems right, but that isn't creative (have you noticed?).

When you try to make everything perfect as you go, whatever you're doing loses what we call "spontaneity." It ends up being stiff and not very natural—definitely not an expression of you. It's kind of like erasing an answer on a test so many times that you rub a hole in the paper. Being a perfectionist doesn't make things perfect. It just makes you think it can never be good enough, that there's always something more you could do to make it perfect, and that takes all the fun out of it.

Try just finishing a project all the way through before you stop to fix things, and see what happens. Ask yourself, "If I didn't have to do them perfectly, what kind of things would I try?" Then just go for it!

🌸 *SUZY: I'd like to make up my own gymnastics routine, but what if it isn't any good? I mean, what if it's dumb and everybody laughs at it? Should I just let the choreographer do it, since she's, like, this professional?*

The first thing you should do is decide to make up your routine just for yourself, for your own pleasure. Don't think of it as something you have to

perform for other people. You might decide to do that later, but for right now, just play around with it by yourself.

Remember as you go that what you come up with might actually be "dumb"—at first. Every work of art needs time to grow, change, and develop. You should try lots of things. Some of it won't work and you'll end up tossing it and trying something else. But eventually, it will all come together and you'll have something you really love (you—not anybody else yet). It may sound weird, but to create something really good you have to be willing to create something that's really bad in the beginning.

🌸 *RENI: When I first started playing the violin, it was fun. I was always writing my own music and playing around with different fingerings and stuff. But then when I had to compete for first chair and All-State Orchestra, it stopped being fun. I don't have time to even think about making up songs because I always have to be better than everybody else in the orchestra. Will it ever be fun again?*

You have fallen into the competition trap. Lots of people get tripped up on that one! Don't misunderstand; a little bit of competition can make us better at what we do. But when it becomes the main thing we think about when we're creating our art—that's not so good. It can make us think things like: What's the point in even trying? and Even if I'm the best right now, somebody's bound to come along who can do it better, and even, I can't stand her. She doesn't really play better than I do—the teacher just gives her all the breaks because she's teacher's pet.

None of that sounds like a God thing, and it isn't. Competing too much takes our thoughts away from the joy of what we're doing—in your case the beautiful music you're making for God—and makes us focus on beating someone else.

Sure you want to be first chair, you want to be chosen for All-State, and you're willing to work for those things. But be sure you're making some time to release your creative side and let it play around with new ideas, which will probably make you a better player anyway. If you aren't chosen for those honors, have a good cry and then go on playing. God has a special plan for you.

❀ *ZOOEY: I think everybody's creative but me. I've tried different stuff. I took this drawing class and my drawings were so lame I quit. I tried out for choir at school, but I didn't make it. I even dropped out of Brownie Scouts because my arts and crafts things always turned out stupid. Even the troop leader thought my clay cow was a turtle. I guess I must be the one person God made who has no creative talent at all.*

Bless your heart! First, you've had some bad experiences, like not being chosen for choir and having your Brownie leader not recognize what you had made. But those things don't mean you can't create. They just mean choir wasn't the best thing for you at the time and your troop leader had an underdeveloped imagination! And who was it that decided your drawings were lame? You, right? How long did you stick with it before you quit? One class? Maybe two? One of the rules God made about creativity is that it requires time. Nobody's stupendous the first time they try something.

Besides, you've only mentioned the things we think of as "art." What about the things you like to do—the things you do often just because you enjoy them? Do you daydream? Do you think about a movie for

several days after you've seen it? When you read a book, can you picture the characters in your mind? If you've answered yes, you have imagination. And imagination is the key to creativity. It's just a matter of discovering your own unique way of creating. That doesn't have to be painting, singing, or making stuff with clay. The whole purpose of this book is to help you find your own special art.

Just Do It

Before we go plunging into a creative project, there are a few things you need to do to get ready. Here we go!

1. Turn off the television!

Watching TV is a fun way to kick back and relax after you've been really busy. But have you noticed that the more television you watch, the more you want to watch? Once you plop yourself down to watch cartoons or old reruns of sitcoms after school, you find yourself watching the next one, and then the next one, and then the next one, until all your free time is gone. It's hard to watch one show and then get up and get out your watercolors or make a tape of all your favorite songs.

The best thing about television is that you can turn it off—so do it. If you don't already have a limit on TV hours at your house, set one for yourself—like only an hour or even a half hour a day—and then ask your mom or dad to help you stick to it. TV doesn't require any imagination on your part, so it doesn't help you be your best creative self. Who needs it?

2. Look at how much you're reading.

If you love to read and you know you have your face in a book more than most people, pay attention to how many hours a day you read, and how many hours you do creative things, either alone or with others. Reading does require imagination, and it can lead to wonderful daydreams that can, in turn, lead you to creative projects and activities. But if you're *always* reading, you may never get to the project—activity—the ideas-of-your-own part. Set aside at least an hour a day for some activity other than reading—something that requires creativity on your part. You're bound to find your own world opening up around you. (Just be sure you finish reading *this* book!)

3. Find your own private place for dreaming up ideas.

Where you actually *do* creative stuff will depend on the kinds of things you decide to do. But before every project or activity there's an idea, and it's good to have a private place where you can be completely yourself so that those ideas can come to you.

Your space should have these features:

• No interruptions—no visitors or telephone calls

- No distractions—radios, televisions, computers, or chattering brothers and sisters
- Comfort—a place where you can really get into the dreaming position
- Music—if music helps you think
- Out of the way—a place where you can feel free and peaceful

Where does a ten-year-old girl find a place like that? Here are some suggestions:

- Your room from 7:00 to 8:00 P.M. You finish your homework and hang a sign on your doorknob that says:

PLEASE DO NOT DISTURB DAYDREAMING IN PROGRESS

- A tree in your backyard
- A corner of your attic
- The garage—behind some boxes
- The bathtub—complete with bubbles and lots of hot water
- The far backseat of the minivan on your way home from school

See? The possibilities are endless!

4. Don't—that is, DO NOT—in other words, Never!—think of your creative time as something you *have* to do!

Weaving more creativity into your life isn't like setting up times for homework, chores, and flossing your teeth. You won't have to "schedule it in" if what you're doing is fun. In fact, if it isn't fun for you—find something else to do! It's okay to dabble until you find something that gives you a boost of enthusiasm.

Talking to God About It

We're going to be doing some creative praying in this book, so stand by for something different in each chapter. Let's start with a Jar Full of Prayers.

- Find a medium-sized jar, like the kind mayonnaise comes in. Get rid of the mayonnaise, of course—clean it all out and strip off the label.

- Decorate your jar any way you want. Think about what prayers look like in your mind and let your design reflect that. You can paint on your jar, cover it with paper, use stickers, or make it fancy with fabric and trims—anything you want. Remember, there is no right or wrong way. Just make it something *you* like.

- Now get yourself some paper that you can cut into strips. Any kind of paper is okay—go plain or colored or printed with a design—it's entirely up to you. Use the strips of paper to write down:

1. Your fears about being creative.
2. Things you'd like to create.
3. Creative activities you'd like to try.
4. Things or people that might stand in your way.
5. Creative things you've dreamed about doing when you "grow up."

- Each day during your prayer time (you do have one, don't you? If not, it's time to create one), draw a slip of paper from your prayer jar and pray about what's written there. If it's a fear, ask God to help you work through it, and then give your fear to God. If it's a dream or a hope, ask God to show you whether it's his will for you. Ask him to help you carry it out if it is. If it's an obstacle that's in your way, ask God to help you find a loving way to get rid of it.

- Put the slip of paper back in the jar after you've prayed. If you draw it out again another day, you'll be surprised at the ways God has already started to answer your prayer.

- Add more slips as other ideas come to you. And remember, there is nothing so small you can't talk to God about it.

Lily Pads give you a chance to ramble on in writing about private topics. You don't have to think about spelling and grammar, and you don't have to share what you've written with anyone else. This is just for you!

What color did God make you? Are you bright sunny yellow, always cheerful and energetic, like daisies and lemon Popsicles? Are you purple, sort of dark and mysterious, like velvet robes and blackberry syrup? Or are you silver, streamlined and sleek, like buttons on a stereo or a shiny CD? Pick the color of *you* and write about yourself as that color. Draw and color in a picture if you want.

This is who I am . . .

Jazzed About Journals

**Since we have these promises, dear friends, let us purify ourselves
from everything that contaminates body and spirit,
perfecting holiness out of reverence for God.**
2 Corinthians 7:1

Pretty diaries and cute journals—you know, those blank books that sometimes have a lock and key on them—often come to girls your age as Christmas or birthday presents. They seem to be the gift of choice of grandmothers and aunts who have kept diaries all their lives and think you should too.

If someone gave you a diary or journal for writing down all your most private thoughts every day (and maybe somebody already has), would you:

Like **Lily,** add it to your already large collection of journals and start using it right away?

Like **Suzy,** write in it every day because you thought you were supposed to, and worry every time about whether you were doing it right?

Like **Kresha,** wonder what you were supposed to do with it?

Like **Reni,** think it's a great idea, except you have too many other things to do.

Like **Zooey,** think, *I'm not the journal-writing type. Why didn't Aunt Maggie send me a gift certificate to a CD store or something?*

If you were or think you might be like any of the Girlz above, this chapter definitely is for you! If you're not including journaling in your daily activities *and* enjoying it, you might be missing out on something not only fun but helpful. And if you're like most of us, you need all the help with creative living you can get!

But why journal? Isn't going to church and doing your best in school and not clobbering your siblings enough to guarantee you a pretty good life? Before we answer that question, let's make sure you know what "journaling" really is.

A *journal* is a blank book you go to every day at about the same time— it's an important part of your daily activities. In that book, you simply fill up one page (more if you want) with anything that comes into your head. That can include:

- What you did yesterday.

- The people in your life—those you're getting along with and those who are making you want to chew your fingernails to the quick.
- Things you're happy about.
- Things you're worried about.
- Things you're afraid of.
- Things you wonder about.
- Things that make you mad.
- Things that bring you to tears.
- Things you hope for.
- Things you're looking forward to.

Your page of writing can include anything you want, even if it's not on this list. There's nothing too silly, lame, dumb, or even whiney to put in your journal.

You can write in your journal any way you want to—get this!—you don't have to worry about spelling, punctuation, capital letters, grammar, or any of that stuff! Those things are only important when you are communicating with other people. Since this journal is for you and you alone, you can write it in code if that tickles your fancy.

If writing is hard for you, you can draw pictures or make designs to represent the things you're thinking about—but once you realize nobody's going to criticize your journal (because nobody's going to see it) you'll probably switch to writing.

We're going to talk more about journal ideas below, but first, let's go back to our question: "Yeah, yeah—sounds great—but why? Why do it?" The answer, as usual, comes from God.

HOW IS THIS A God Thing?

In one of his letters to the Christians in Corinth, Paul urged them to get rid of all the things that stood between them and God—the things that distracted them or even led them to do godless things. He told them to make their whole lives as pure as holy temples (2 Corinthians 7:1).

But exactly how do you do that? How do you dump all that yucky stuff so you can get on with living a life full of God—which we've already figured out includes being creative like he is?

Writing in a journal every day is one way to do that. Whining, griping, worrying, and even hoping for something in particular can stand between you and your ability to be creative like God intended. (It can also be an obstacle between you and a lot of other God things. But since we're focusing on creativity in this book, we'll just be talking about that.) When you get it all out on paper, it doesn't follow you around all the time, clinging to you like a sticky cobweb. You get all that negative stuff out of the way and open your mind to a whole new world of creativity.

And, writing in a journal—where spelling and capitalization and all that stuff doesn't count—lets you work without the fear of criticism. No one— not even you—will be reading what you write and saying, "This is trash! What were you thinking?" God *really* likes that. Jesus even told his followers, "Do not judge, or you too will be judged" (Matthew 7:1), and that includes you! Writing in a journal where you don't pick on yourself the whole time gives you practice for when you're doing a creative project. You will be able to get out of your own way.

Here are some more ways writing in a journal is a God thing. It's easy to see why God wants these things to happen!

- You can write yourself out of a really cranky mood.
- You can clear your head so you can hear God's voice instead of just yours all the time.
- You can learn to think with the whole brain God gave you, not just the side that's logical and helps you remember how to multiply and how to spell your name.

- You can learn things about yourself that you didn't know before— either things you can now use as God things or things you can ask God to help you get control over.

Girlz WANT TO KNOW

You might still have some questions about how this all works and why you should take the time to try it. The Girlz definitely did, so maybe the answers to their questions will help you.

✿ *SUZY: I don't even know how to start writing in a journal. I still keep thinking I'm going to do it wrong or it's going to be stupid and not make me creative at all.*

Suzy, writing in a journal isn't going to make you creative; you're already creative. Journal writing is just going to let you be the creative person you are. There truly isn't a right or wrong way to do it, unless you're acting like an editor the whole time, constantly correcting yourself. Lots of people have a little trouble getting started. Here are some ideas that might help you:

- Start by writing about what happened to you the day before. You can tell all the stuff you can remember or just a few important things. Sometimes, writing about one thing will cause you to start thinking about something else. Say you're writing about how you had eggplant for dinner the night before, and you hate eggplant, and that gets you thinking about a lot of foods you don't particularly care for. List all the foods you can't stand, and then maybe go on to list the ones you *do* like. That may lead you to write about how you'd like to learn to cook, because if you did you'd make ... See how it works? Letting your mind wander into the possibilities when you're journaling helps you to do the same thing when you're planning a project.
- Play some music while you're journaling and write about how it makes you feel.

- Make a wish list.
- Write about "what if?" What if you had a tail? What if you had to give a name to each one of your toes? What if you found $100,000 in cash in a backpack? What if you could fly? Wherever those "what-ifs" lead you is where you should go in your journal.

✿ *RENI: This journal thing sounds really cool, but I have so much other stuff going on, I really don't have time to add one more thing.*

But, Reni, you can't afford not to! Writing in a journal can help make all those other things you do so much better. Try getting up just fifteen minutes earlier in the morning to write in your journal. Skip that last TV show you watch at night, and write then. Don't dawdle so much over your chores so you can use the extra time for journaling.

When you get into it and start enjoying it, you'll always find the time. By the way, if your schedule is that full and you're twelve years old or younger, it might be good to look at how many activities you're involved in. Having too much to do when you're still technically a kid isn't always healthy. Do you really need to be on two sports teams, take gymnastics and piano lessons, and belong to 4-H, Girl Scouts, and three church groups? Think about it.

✿ *KRESHA: Writing is really hard for me. Even when I know that no one else will read it, I have such a hard time I almost end up crying.*

That's a bummer, Kresha. The first thing to do—which has nothing to do with journaling—is make sure you're getting plenty of help with your reading at school or from some adult. Maybe, for example, there's a retired schoolteacher at your church who would be glad to tutor you once a week after school. Writing is such a fun thing and such an important skill for your education, it's something you want to feel comfortable doing.

Now, when it comes to journaling, the whole point is to enjoy having a conversation with yourself and write it down. If at first those conversations happen in pictures, doodle in your journal for a page. Or just list words you like the sound of. Or list the people you love, then make a list of people you really like and want to get to know better. List the people you're having a hard time with and wish you weren't. For extra fun, try getting yourself some different colored pens or pencils. Think of more lists to write, then decorate them. Pretty soon this writing thing will get easier and you'll try phrases and then sentences. But remember, writing in your journal is all about freeing yourself to be creative. Don't turn it into work!

✿ *ZOOEY: My mom doesn't like me to keep secrets. If I keep this private journal, she's going to say I shouldn't have anything to hide. If it can't be totally private, I don't want to do it.*

You know, Zooey, we always tell you that your parents have the last word. But your mom might change her "last word" if you explain to her that you're not hiding anything—you just need a place to sort things out, things other people might think are silly. They're not bad things—they're just private things. If that doesn't work, encourage her to read this chapter. If she still doesn't quite see it your way, you can keep a journal where you only write things you're not embarrassed for anybody else to read. At least that will get you comfortable with journaling. Then after about a month, you can discuss it with your mom again—maybe let her read what you've written. Until she gives the okay, don't try to hide your journal from your mom. If she finds it, she isn't going to trust you. In these growing-up years, a lot of what you do is build trust with your mom and dad. Sometimes it's a slow process, but it'll be worth it. Someday you'll be able to keep private, secret papers and know they're for your eyes only—and you'll already know how to write them!

❀ *LILY: My mom says I already spend way too much time in my room by myself writing. But I love doing it. Why do I have to go join the family for some dumb game if I'd rather be journaling?*

It's important to live a balanced life, Lil, and journaling will help you do that. As you're writing in your journal, you'll hear yourself wishing for adventure or longing for something exciting to happen. Pay attention to that—it's telling you to get out of that room on a regular basis, like your mom says, so that exciting adventures can happen. Sit down with your mom and talk about how much time you can agree is reasonable for you to spend alone. Let her know that board games aren't your idea of a fun time with the family, and suggest some ways you might actually like spending time with your parents and siblings. And remember, too much of any good thing isn't healthy for you.

Just Do It

Got the idea? Then let's get started!

1. Get yourself a notebook of some kind for your journal. There are lots of ways to set it up, and none of them involves spending a lot of money (moms like that!). Here are some ideas:

(a) Buy one of those blank books they sell in stationery sections and bookstores.

(b) Buy a spiral or some other pad of paper and decorate it any way you wish.

(c) Get a binder, fill it with notebook paper, and decorate the cover to reflect you.

(d) Get some notebook paper and two sheets of construction paper and staple it all together, with the colored paper being your front and back covers—decorated, of course!

2. Collect, preferably from around the house, the pens and/or pencils you want to use for writing in your journal. Find some neat way to keep them together with your journal. Maybe you have one of those pencil containers that goes into a binder. Perhaps you can decorate an empty can and put your writing instruments in that. Or see if your mom has an old makeup bag with a zipper—perfect for a selection of writing tools.

3. Decide where your journaling spot is going to be. You don't have to go to that same spot every day, of course. It might even be fun to try lots of different sites for this part of your day. Most people, though, like to know they're going to meet themselves in the same place. It can even be in that same dreaming spot you picked out in chapter one.

4. Decide when your best journaling time will be and try to write in your journal at that time every day. You might have to do something a little different on the weekends or make exceptions when things come up that you can't control—like dentist appointments and stuff. Even so, a regular journaling time will help you stick with it, especially at first when it's still new. Do it for two weeks and it'll become a habit!

5. Unless your parents (like Zooey's mom) have a problem with you having privacy, keep your journal in a safe place where it won't be a temptation to someone casually walking through. Again, it's not as if you're hiding anything, but you want to feel free to express your fears and doubts and secret hopes. You won't do that if you think your little brother is going to be able to snoop in it. If it's brothers and sisters you're concerned about—rather than parents—write anything that's really secret in code. Sounds like fun, doesn't it?

6. Now that you have everything set up, you're ready to start journaling. If you're having trouble getting started, refer back to the answer to Suzy's letter in this chapter. If you're really, really having trouble, invite some of your friends over and make journals together. Brainstorm for fun stuff to write about until you get the hang of it. You can check with each other at a get-together now and then to encourage everyone to keep at it. Sharing is allowed, but only if the writer wants to share. And no fair coaxing someone into it! Respect is way important.

7. After you've been writing in your journal for two weeks, go back and read what you've written. It's fun to use a yellow marker to highlight things like:

(a) Ideas you've come up with.
(b) Things you'd like to try ("I want to ask my dad if I can have a corner of his veggie garden for my own plants this summer").

(c) Things you want to do better ("I feel really bad when I yell at Sissy—I wish I wouldn't do that").

(d) Discoveries you've made ("We wrote poems in school today—and I'm really good at it!").

Then go for it. Let your journal be like the springs in a diving board that propels you up and out. The creativity pool is just waiting for you to dive in.

Talking to God About It

Since we've talked so much about drawing in a journal (that's called "visual journaling"), why not try drawing a prayer?

Go to a quiet place. Get comfortable. Close your eyes and get very quiet. Ask God, either out loud or silently, to show you what you need to pray about. Ask if he wants you to give thanks or ask for something, either for yourself or for somebody else. Ask if he'd like for you to confess something to him that you've been holding back, if he wants you to offer some service, or if he just wants to hear how much you love him.

When you have an idea what it is, think about what that looks like in pictures. Thanking him for your mom who is being so cool about helping you through a tough time might look like a drawing of your mom or a heart or a huge decorated "Thank You!" Asking him to help you get along better with your soccer coach might come out as a picture of your face in a soccer ball, smiling at Coach. Just needing to praise him could be a design of gorgeous colors. See how that works?

Then "pray" your work of art. Put it where you can see it (since God will see it no matter where you put it!) and let it be a reminder to pray that prayer often. One day you'll look at it and realize your prayer has been answered. Then maybe it's time for another work of art for God!

If I could have the perfect time and place to journal, it would be . . .

Creative Adventures

Many, O LORD my God, are the wonders you have done.
The things you planned for us no one can recount to you;
were I to speak and tell of them, they would be too many to declare.
Psalm 40:5

So far as we've talked about creativity, we've focused on the "inside" things you can do to find out just how creative you are. But ideas and inspiration don't just come from your head. A lot of it happens when you're out there getting life all over you—having adventures in living.

If you're really honest about it, and if you don't consider things like money and time and permission from your parents or even your own fears, which of these things would you rather do?

- Read about riding in a hot-air balloon or actually go up in one?
- Watch a special on TV about tiger cubs or get to play with some for real?
- Listen to your friend tell you about the fashion show she went to or go to one yourself?
- See *The Prince of Egypt* five times or visit the pyramids up close and personal?

Most of us would rather *do* than just *hear about*. In fact, even when it comes to our journey with God, the Bible tells us to be "doers of the word," not just hearers (James 1:22–25 KJV). It works in our creative lives too. As often as we can get out there and "get some of it on us," we need to do it.

What exactly do we mean by this getting-some-of-it-on-us thing? Do we have to have a lot of money? Do we have to have parents who will drop everything to fly us to an African jungle one day and the Great Wall of China the next? Do we have to be completely fearless—willing to bungee jump and scuba dive and ride Class 5 rapids all by ourselves?

Uh—NO!

To have creative adventures, you don't have to be rich or blessed with world-traveling parents or even be brave enough to leave your own town. All you need is a little imagination, at least an hour a week, and sometimes some help from your family.

A creative adventure is simply that one time during your busy week that you use for treating your artistic self to something fun—something that intrigues you and has nothing to do with school or chores or any of your other responsibilities. It's just a little activity that makes your imagination happy—just the way getting a double scoop of Rocky Road on a waffle cone might make your taste buds happy or putting your favorite song on repeat on the CD player might make your ears happy. Some examples probably would help:

Lily found a trunk in her grandmother's attic. Mudda gave Lily permission to explore it, and she spent a whole summer afternoon going back into the past. It was a blast for Lily.

Reni was at a yard sale with her mom and found a tape of nothing but violin solos. Since she's nuts over playing the violin herself, she used her allowance to buy it and spent two hours that day listening to the tape while munching grapes and imagining herself as the soloist. It was the best for Reni.

Kresha heard on the radio on the way to school that the city was going to blow up a building downtown on Saturday. She got excited and asked her mom if they could go. Mom was up for it, so they went, taking along her little brothers. It was awesome for Kresha.

Suzy found out that the next-door neighbor's Irish setter had given birth to puppies. She asked if she could spend some time playing with them. The neighbor was more than happy to let her, so Suzy first read a short book on Irish setters, packed some treats for the mama dog, and spent an hour and a half the next Saturday with six little red mini-dogs. It was a blessing for Suzy.

Zooey loves the sewing and crafts section of Wal-Mart, but when she's shopping with her mom, Mom is always in a hurry and Zooey doesn't get to spend as much time there as she would like. One Saturday, when she'd done all her chores and her mom started to give Zooey her allowance, Zooey asked if her mom would take her to Wal-Mart instead and let her spend an hour just looking in the arts and crafts department. It was awesome for Zooey.

So you see, a "creative adventure" is just a short block of time—maybe an hour or two—set aside *on purpose* just to exercise your creative self. You use that time to do something that makes you happy, gives you ideas or energy, or is just plain joy. A creative adventure is just a short, simple outing that fills you up. Although you're just having a good time, this adventure is busy feeding your creativity in the same way veggies nourish your body and studying Scripture enriches your soul. How does that work? It's a God thing—of course.

HOW IS THIS A **God Thing?**

The writer of the Psalms must have been pretty good at getting life on him, because he talked a lot about the cool things he discovered when he got out there and experienced it:

How priceless is your unfailing love! Both high and low among men find refuge in the shadow of your wings. They feast on the abundance of your house; you give them drink from your river of delights. For with you is the fountain of life; in your light we see light.
Psalm 36:7–9

Many, O LORD my God, are the wonders you have done. The things you planned for us no one can recount to you; were I to speak and tell of them, they would be too many to declare.
Psalm 40:5

Blessed are those you choose and bring near to live in your courts! We are filled with the good things of your house, of your holy temple.
Psalm 65:4

Great are the works of the LORD; they are pondered by all who delight in them. Glorious and majestic are his deeds, and his righteousness endures forever.
Psalm 111:2–3

One generation will commend your works to another; they will tell of your mighty acts. They will speak of the glorious splendor of your majesty, and I will meditate on your wonderful works.
Psalm 145:4–5

My heart is steadfast, O God; I will sing and make music with all my soul. Awake, harp and lyre! I will awaken the dawn.
Psalm 108:1–2

We spend a lot of time in Sunday school, church, and Bible study learning how we're supposed to live decent, righteous lives—and we definitely need to do that. We'd be a mess otherwise. But we often overlook the fact that God wants us to have some fun along the way—get some enjoyment out of this life that he has given us.

That's what you do when you set aside time for creative adventures where you relax and stretch out your imagination to fill up the places inside that have gotten drained out. You enjoy God's world and the things he has inspired other creative people to make, so at the same time you enjoy God himself. He wants us to do that, because while we're out there picking strawberries, collecting seashells, or going to Dad's office with him on a Saturday, God is enjoying *you*. The psalmist writes, "For the LORD takes delight in his people" (Psalm 149:4).

Something mysterious happens when you take the time to look for God with your eyes wide open. You do that, of course, by reading the Bible, by praying, by writing in journals, by serving the church and the community.

You also do it when you're having a creative adventure. The mysterious result? You start to feel good—as if you're strolling at leisure with God in the sunlit fields of life. You start to feel more confident that you're doing God things and that God is really working in you, stirring up your sleepy creativity 'til it's wide awake. "Blessed are those whose strength is in you, who have set their hearts on pilgrimage (Psalm 84:5). When you travel on the same road with God, he makes all things possible. (See Matthew 19:26.)

If that's still hard to understand, just think of it this way: Writing in your journal is like praying; a creative adventure is like being on the alert for the answers to those prayers.

CHECK Yourself OUT

So now you're ready to get out there and fill yourself up with the way things smell, taste, feel, sound, and look. You're ready to do some things just because they're delightful, because they're interesting, because they're just plain fun—for *you*. One of the important "rules" of taking a creative adventure is that you take it either by yourself or with as few other people as possible so you can do and see and taste and smell what's fun for you. (There are plenty of times when you need to think about other people's wishes. It's okay to take one or two hours a week just for you.) So how do you know what to do? Let's find out. It's quiz time!

Write the answers to these questions. Don't forget to use the most fun pen or pencil you can find. *Do* forget to worry about spelling—just like in your journal!

As you answer the questions, don't consider things like cost or time or whether you could actually pull it off. Just consider your joy. (It's a God thing!)

- What are your five favorite games to play (anything from soccer to Go Fish, or hide-and-seek to Keep-the-Frisbee-Away-from-the-Dog)?

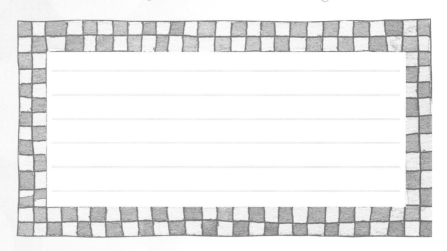

- What are your five most treasured possessions?

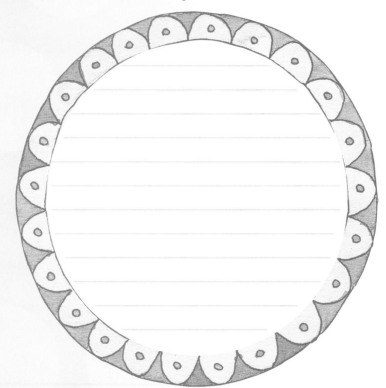

- **What are your five favorite books?**

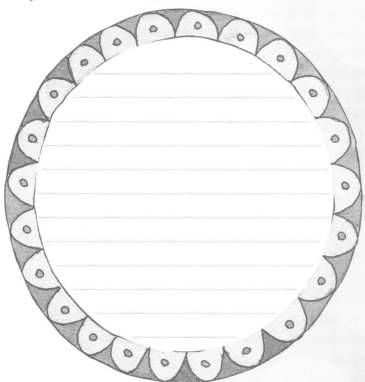

- **Who are five famous people, either alive or dead, whom you admire?**

- List five hobbies you already enjoy or you think you'd like.

- What are your five favorite places (places you've been or dream of visiting)?

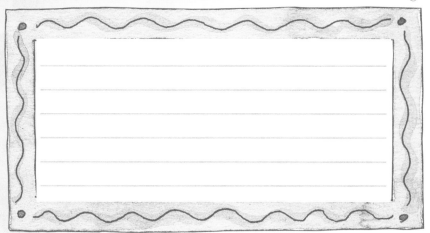

Just Do It

So what do all these lists you've made tell you? They give you hints for taking your own creative adventures!

You can turn any "favorite" into an adventure by following these guidelines:

- It costs little or no money.
- It doesn't take longer than two hours.

- You can do it alone or with no more than a few other people who want to do it too.
- It would be *way* fun for you.

The best way to explain how this works is to look at the way Lily turned one of her lists into creative adventures. Here's her list of five favorite places:

☆ Moorestown, N.J. (a historic town very close to where she lives)
☆ Any beach
☆ London (a place she's never been but would love to visit)
☆ New York City (she's only been there once)
☆ A Native American pueblo (never been—wants to go)

And here are the creative adventures she concocted from her list:

✳ Since her dad likes to go to Moorestown too, she asked him if they could go there for their next father-daughter outing and if she could choose three things she wanted to do while there. They saw the Friends' School, had real ice-cream sundaes in an old-fashioned ice-cream parlor, and spent a whole hour in an antique shop.
✳ She created a little beach corner in the backyard, complete with beach chair, cooler of sodas, and suntan lotion, and sat out there looking at the photo albums full of pictures of the Robbins's many summers on the Jersey shore.
✳ She called a local travel agent (with her mom's permission, of course) and asked the agent to send her travel information about London. With the posters and brochures they sent, she set up a London corner in her room and spent a whole afternoon in it, drinking tea and reading books on London she'd checked out of the library. Now she visits her London corner whenever she gets a craving for Jolly Old England.
✳ She found a recipe for New York–style cheesecake and, with her grandmother's help, made her own. She and Mudda set up their own New York café in the kitchen and dug in.

✳ She found out there was an exhibit about American Pueblo Indians at the local museum. No one in Lily's family wanted to go, but Reni and her mom did, so the three of them went together. Lily took her saved-up allowance with her and bought some for-real moccasins in the gift shop.

Now look at your lists of favorites. Can you come up with "almost there" ways to put some adventure into those things you love? Try it with your first list here. And remember, low cost, short time, just big enough for you and maybe a friend or two, and *fun* for you! If you have trouble getting started, get a fun person with a good imagination to help.

_____

_____

_____

_____

_____

Girlz WANT TO KNOW

This all sounds like a pretty good idea, but what if you run into things that stand in your way? It happens, but there are ways to work it out:

❀ *LILY: My family already thinks I'm Loony Tunes. If I start talking about creative adventures, they're really going to think I've lost my marbles!*

A lot of times we don't bring up the fun ideas we have for stuff to do because we're afraid other people are going to think we're silly. That's a shame. In the first place, no idea you have is dumb or lame if it sounds fun to you. In the second place, when people make fun of you for dreaming up something out of the ordinary, they definitely aren't taking your feelings into consideration. But since we can't expect to change other people, we sometimes have to work around them.

Start with creative adventures you can do by yourself or at least without involving your family members. If they ask you why you're using all your dog-walking money to buy a starter set for an herb garden on your bedroom windowsill, you don't have to go into a long explanation about creativity and creative adventures. Just tell them you're doing it because you want to (using only the friendliest of tones, of course!). That isn't hiding anything—it's heading off the teasing before it has a chance to start.

Once you've gotten into the creative adventure habit and you'd like to venture outside the yard, try taking the most understanding member of your family aside and discussing it with him or her. If your dad, for instance, gets the creative adventure thing, he'll also get why you don't want to be the brunt of all the jokes at the dinner table about it. Beyond that, sometimes we just have to learn to say, "It's okay if you laugh. I am unique!" When teasers don't get a response from you, they usually move on.

✿ *RENI: Every creative adventure I've come up with has to do with orchestra and the violin. Is that bad?*

It's definitely not "bad." How cool that you have an art you're passionate about! Go ahead, see concerts, visit music stores, and pretend you're conducting while listening to a Mozart CD. But while you're enjoying God in those ways, keep your eyes and ears open for other things that strike your fancy. Maybe when you're at a concert you'll see a poster for a ballet. Wouldn't it be neat to go to Suzy's next dance recital?

It's good to create balance in your life so you're not focused on just one thing every minute. We all need a little reading, a little music, a little physical exercise, a little quiet, a little fellowship, and a little zaniness. Being sure you have all those things will only make you a better musician.

✿ *KRESHA: We don't have extra money at my house. I don't even get an allowance. I don't think I can have creative adventures.*

Yes, you can! After all, creative adventures aren't supposed to cost a lot of money, and if you use none, so much the better. That just means you'll need to use more imagination than somebody with bucks to spend.

Let's say one of your favorite possessions is the Walkman your mom got you for Christmas. Can you check tapes out of the public library? Can you choose some that help you learn another language? Or some with music from a country you'd love to visit? And while you're listening to your tapes, can you surround yourself with books from the library about that country? Can you put together a costume from stuff in your closet to put you in the mood? Does the music make you want to get up and dance? Do it! Become an expert on that country—and then try another country or culture. What a blast—and you haven't spent a penny!

✿ *ZOOEY: I've done a bunch of creative adventures at home and I'm ready to get out of here! I want to see a play in a real theater, look at the tropical birds at the pet shop, and look at the old tombstones in St. Mary's cemetery. But my mom's too busy to take me, and she won't let me go alone. She also says if I ask her one more time, she's gonna ground me. Just when I thought I was gonna get to be creative after all.*

It sounds like you have some great ideas. It's a bummer that your mom isn't available to enjoy those things with you. Parents are busier these days than they've ever been, so it's easy to see why they'd have trouble squeezing one more thing into their schedules. But don't give up creativity!

There are a couple of things you can do. First, let your friends know what things you'd like to do. Chances are they'd like to do the same things, and perhaps their parents would provide transportation and chaperoning. It's not

the kind of thing you ask your friends' moms to do, but just making it known that you have ideas will sometimes jiggle somebody into offering.

Another way to go at it is to think about the things your mom is already doing and see if you can fit your adventure into those errands. Is the tropical bird store in the same shopping center as the grocery store? Can you negotiate five minutes in there before you two go for groceries—with your promise to carry all the bags into the house when you get home? Once you've taken a few adventurous trips outside your house in those ways and talked about how much fun you've had—and how much you'd like to share that with Mom—she may even want to fit some into her schedule after all. Use some patience—don't nag. Be creative! The adventures you do get to have will be that much more fun for you when they happen.

Talking to God About It

Since we've talked about *doing* in this chapter, let's pray an *action prayer* this time. What could you *do* to help you focus on God as you talk to him? Here are some suggestions, but feel free to be creative and think up your own.

- Light a candle (with a grown-up's permission) and pray by its glow. As you blow it out, ask God to be the light that shines in you for the rest of the day.
- Sing your favorite praise song. Make up your own words if you want to. Maybe you can fit them to the things you're praying about.
- Does someone you know have sign language skills? Have him or her teach you how to sign a simple prayer.
- Write a poem for God and decorate it. Put it up in the place where you talk to God or keep it folded in your Bible.
- Do whatever you do best as a prayer of thanksgiving for your skills. Bake cookies. Tap dance. Make the baby laugh. Whistle. Make a friendship bracelet. As you work, pay attention. You probably will feel God's pleasure.

If I had the time, money, and chaperone to have a great creative adventure, I would ...

Imaginary Lives

**Teach us to number our days aright,
that we may gain a heart of wisdom.**
Psalm 90:12

If you asked Lily what she wants to be when she "grows up," it probably would take her a good half hour to answer you—not because she couldn't think of anything, but because she has so many possibilities cooking in her brain:

- model
- doctor
- professional party giver
- newspaper columnist
- political activist
- actress
- forest ranger
- public speaker

You get the idea. Even if she lived as long as Noah, she couldn't do all of those things—at least, not for a living. But she—and you—could live a pretty creative life if you *played* at those professions for fun.

Lily likes the idea of being a fashion model, but she doesn't want to devote her whole life to it. If she just wanted to play with modeling for fun, though, she could:

- Go to some fashion shows, like the ones that are sometimes held in malls for free.
- Dress her friends up and have a photo shoot right in the backyard.
- Read fashion magazines at the library and play with some of the models' poses at home (out of sight of her little brother!).
- Suggest to her youth group leader that the youth group or Sunday school class put on a fashion show for a fund-raiser; she'd volunteer to help organize it, of course!

In other words, Lily can have a great time *and* be creative by "acting out imaginary lives." She *might* find out in the midst of it all that she really has a dream of pursuing one of those professions on her list, but that isn't the point of the imaginary life activity. It's just a, well, a game she—and you—can play to help rustle up creative ideas and bring out those gifts you didn't even know you had.

Some Christians get a little nervous when talk turns to having your own dreams and going after them. Aren't we supposed to find out what God wants for our lives and then follow his will?

Yes—but why don't we see if we can figure out just exactly what that means?

HOW IS THIS A God Thing?

The Old Testament is full of stories about people who were busy minding their own business—tending sheep, that kind of thing—when God came to them with an idea he wanted them to carry out. We're talking about Noah, Moses, David, Jonah, and that whole crowd. None of them ever *dreamed* of doing the kind of creative work God had planned for them. That's the way it works sometimes.

But at other times in the Bible, we see people who went to God with an idea and he blessed them with the desires of their hearts.

- Abram and Sarai wanted a son, and that happened to be what God had in mind—enough descendants to outnumber the stars.
- Hannah also wanted to be a mom, and God gave her Samuel. It worked out for both of them. Hannah promised to dedicate any child she bore to God, and God needed a prophet just about then!
- Solomon had all kinds of great political ideas that brought a lot of old fighting tribes together. God seemed to love that (at least until Solomon started thinking he could do anything he wanted—but that's another story).
- John the Baptist grew up knowing he wanted to pave the way for the Messiah, and God definitely approved of that journey.

- Remember the lady who had been sick for years and wanted nothing more than to be healed? Jesus just felt her touch him and she was made well.
- And some of those first disciples, Andrew and Simon (Peter), were already looking for the man who had the "truth" when John the Baptist pointed Jesus out to Andrew, and he went after Jesus and told his brother to come too.

You may already be saying, "But didn't Abram and Hannah and Solomon and John the Baptist and Andrew think of those things because God gave them those wishes and dreams?"

Exactly.

The same is true for all of us. We're not used to thinking that God's will for us and our own inner dreams and hopes could be the same thing—but who do you think *put* those hopes and dreams in your mind in the first place?

Of course, not everything that comes into your mind comes from God. We have evil to deal with in the world too. But if a dream or an idea of yours doesn't go against what the Bible says, it's worth praying about to find out if perhaps that dream is God's dream *for* us.

Yes, Paul tells us in the New Testament that we should "deny ourselves." But he doesn't say, "Deny yourself everything!" He means we need to deny ourselves those things that stand between God and us. If taking art classes or working on a play at school takes up so much of your time that you don't have space in your day for quiet time with God, then you do need to deny yourself some of that. If you're using *all* your spending money for paintbrushes, camera film, or supplies for making earrings and don't have any left to put in the offering plate at church, then you need to do some denying.

The best rule of thumb is: if God comes first in every way in your life, and the things you dream of are in obedience to him, chances are your dream and God's are the same. He definitely likes it when we go after the ideas he gives us.

CHECK Yourself OUT

Want to try the "Imaginary Lives" game for yourself? On the lines below, write down five lives you'd like to live. Write them down as fast as you can without thinking about them too much. If you're still not sure about this, Suzy's and Reni's lists might help you.

_____

_____

_____

_____

_____

SUZY

Professional soccer player

Olympic gymnast

Chemist discovering a cure for cancer

Photographer of wild animals

Astronaut

RENI

Professional violinist

Backup singer

Evening gown designer

Orchestra conductor

FBI agent

Now it's your turn, girl! Think *fun! Exciting! Creative!* Think it from the bottom of your heart!

Look back at your list and be *sure* the "lives" you've written down are ones you'd *really* love to get to do someday. Then read further—because you're going to learn how to make a little bit of "someday" happen today.

Just Do It

Choose one of the "imaginary lives" on your list, the one that sounds like the most *fun* to you. We're not necessarily talking about something brave and noble here—like being a missionary to darkest Africa or being a substitute teacher—unless that's genuinely your idea of a good time. You're not planning your life's work—you're letting your creativity blossom.

Now, think about ways you might dabble in a piece of that life without spending a lot of money or traveling far. A look at Suzy's and Reni's ideas might help.

Suzy chose photographer of wild animals. Her "dabble list" looked like this:

- Get old magazines from Grandpa and cut out pictures of wild animals to put in a scrapbook.
- Check out books on wild animals from the library.
- Use money from recycling cans to buy a disposable camera.
- Take pictures of wild animals I know—Zooey's brother's snake, the squirrels that come to our bird feeders, and the macaw at the beauty shop where we get our hair cut.
- Ask to go to the zoo for my birthday; take pictures there.

Here's Reni's "dabble list" for backup singer:

- Listen to all the backups on my favorite CDs and learn their parts.
- Play around with my dad's tape recorder that has a microphone (with his permission, of course).
- Use my birthday money to make one of those karaoke records at the mall.
- Get the Girlz together and do a song for the school talent show. Kresha has the best voice—she could sing lead, and I could teach the other Girlz the backup. We could have cool costumes and dance steps and everything.

Remember that there is no "right" or "wrong" to this game as long as you follow these guidelines:

1. There's no need to spend money unless you want to, and then it should be your own money (no begging allowed!).
2. Be sure you're putting God first before you plan your dabbling.
3. Keep it fun. If you start getting snappy and frustrated about it, slow down and back off a little. Remember—this is a game!

Ready to give it a shot?

Choose your "imaginary life" from your list:

_____

Write three ways you could dabble in it, following the guidelines above:

1. _____

2. _____

3. _____

Wait—we're not finished yet! *Now* choose one of those ideas from the "dabble list" you just wrote:

_____

Plan how you're going to do that this coming week:
Now—just do it!

Girlz WANT TO KNOW

While **Lily, Reni, and Suzy** were off dabbling, **Zooey** and **Kresha** were bummed out because they both had the same question: What if I can't think of a single way to "dabble?"

This helped them, and maybe it will make this easier for you too.

Choose that one "life" that sounds like the most fun, perhaps nature woman or pilot. Then get yourself some magazines that you're allowed to cut up, some scissors, glue, and a big piece of paper or poster board. Even the cutout side of an old cardboard box will do.

Sit down with your supplies and pull out any pictures that remind you of your "imaginary life." If you're looking for nature woman stuff, any pictures of animals, flowers, trees, and oceans would work, as well as shots of people hiking, camping, running through fields, planting gardens. If pilot is your thing, you'll snatch up pictures of airplanes, airports, suitcases, the sky, clouds, and anything that looks like complicated control boards.

Once you have your stack of pictures, arrange them on your poster board or paper any way you want. The only "rule" is that you like the way it all looks when it's laid out. Then glue your pictures down.

Once it's dry, put your collage (that's what it's called) where you can look at it and enjoy it. Imagine yourself in it smelling, tasting, feeling, hearing, and seeing all that neat stuff. Right there, you're already dabbling. The longer the poster stays in sight, the more likely you are to get ideas from it.

Wouldn't it be fun, Nature Woman, to collect real leaves and find out their names instead of just looking at them in pictures?

Wouldn't it be fun, Pilot Girl, to start a model airplane collection? (Who says that's only for boys?) Turn that old leather jacket in the attic into a flight jacket for yourself (with Mom and Dad's permission). Fly a kite??

Give it a try!

Talking to God About It

In whatever way you choose—drawing, painting, writing a poem or song lyrics, making a collage (remember that the creative possibilities are endless)—describe for God the life you would like to live for him. First, think about it very carefully, probably in your quiet place. Let your ideas come from what you've learned about him and from the thoughts that are the most true to the "you" God made you to be. We're not talking about our imaginary fun lives or our hoped-for careers. We're talking about the kind of *person* you want to be for God. Create that picture as your prayer that he will guide you and bless you along the way.

When I imagine myself as a grown-up, I dream of being a . . .

Partners in Play

**I wash my hands in innocence, and go about your altar, O LORD,
proclaiming aloud your praise and telling of all your wonderful deeds.**
Psalm 26:6–7

A lot of the things we've talked about so far are things you can think about and even do by yourself. You definitely have to know who you are and what you like to do, or you can never be genuinely creative.

But that doesn't mean that creative stuff is a lonely business! So much of what Jesus teaches is about loving each other, working things out with each other, putting other people ahead of us when it's appropriate to do that. That goes for our creative lives too.

Just think about it. How else would plays get performed ... or songs get played by bands ... or beautiful buildings get built ... or books get published? Even in your own creative day, what fun is that cool game you came up with for the playground if nobody else is around to play it with you and make it even cooler? How easy would it be to do a puppet show for your little sister's birthday all by yourself? Why would you even want to *start* dreaming up a backyard circus or a hat-making party or a giant chalk mural on the driveway if you thought you would have to do it all alone? Some things were just meant for people to do together.

Even if we don't want to do our actual creating with someone else, we almost always want to share what we've created with another person. Would you write a story you thought was pretty good and then just stick it in a drawer? Would you make unique friendship bracelets and keep them all in your jewelry box? Would you map out a cool bicycle obstacle course just so you could stare at the map? A *big* part of the creating process is sharing your work with other people. We do create things to give ourselves joy, but that joy is empty if we don't eventually let other folks feel it too.

Besides, we need encouragement when we're creating. We need someone to say, "Wow! That is *so* cool!" or at least, "Now that's interesting. Tell me where you're going with it." Part of that encouragement is just knowing you have friends who are creating too. Together, you can know you're not weirdos because you choose to build a fort or make Roman togas out of bed sheets instead of parking yourself in front of the TV or roaming the mall.

Sounds like a God thing, doesn't it?

HOW IS THIS A God Thing?

In the Bible, God never asked anybody to do any creative act for him all alone.

For instance, he had Aaron help Moses find creative ways to approach Pharaoh. Later it was Joshua who was there to pitch in when the Israelites got whiny. And when the whole creative thing of organizing a new nation got to be too much, God told Moses to get somebody from each family to take some of the load off of him.

Even Jesus didn't do it alone! He picked twelve men and trained them immediately to go out and start spreading this creative new message he'd brought. Not just one man, but a dozen. We have evidence that they bickered among themselves like brothers ("Okay, who forgot the bread?" and "I want to be first!" " No, I get to be first!"), but in the end they stuck together—and look what happened. They called it The Way. We call it Christianity.

It only makes sense that the same guideline applies to us: Creativity is not completely an alone-thing. Paul goes on about that (a lot!) in his first letter to the people in Corinth. Here's what he said:

"There are different kinds of gifts, but the same Spirit. There are different kinds of service, but the same Lord" (1 Corinthians 12:4–5). He goes on to compare everyone's creative gifts to parts of the body—all working together (1 Corinthians 12:12).

While he's on the subject of being like parts of the body, he reminds the Corinthians that God gave each of them a particular gift, but no one gift is more important than anybody else's gift. One of the good things about people working together on a creative project is that they realize how important each person is to the finished product. No one of them could do it alone. No one gets to brag or feel superior. Pretty clever of God, huh?

Paul was so excited about this idea of working together, he told them to "Follow the way of love and eagerly desire spiritual gifts" (1 Corinthians 14:1). Every creative thing we do needs to be done out of love—and not just love of self! He told them that when they got together to worship, each one of them ought to be prepared with something that would be useful to everyone there (1 Corinthians 14:26–27).

And then Paul told them the most important thing of all about creating—prayer. Creativity is delightful and fun, but we also need prayer as we plunge into it—just like we do for every part of our lives.

Just Do It

So what do we mean by "creating together" and being "partners in play?" It can mean a lot of fun stuff!

1. **You can team up with friends who like to do the same kinds of creative things that you do and work on projects together**. Do several of you like drama? Wouldn't it be cool to put together a simple play to perform for your parents? Do a bunch of you have different talents that you could put together to plan a surprise Mother's Day party for all your moms? Or do you and your best friend both love crafts? Maybe you could work together to create your masks for that costume party you've both been invited to? Those kinds of things go so much better when more great minds are involved.

2. **You can get your friends together in a place where you can all work on your**

own individual projects. Maybe it's a craft day, or a sewing bee, or an afternoon when one person is illustrating her poems, another person is doing origami, and still another is making a weather station to put in the backyard. You can encourage each other, help each other when somebody needs an extra finger, and even make suggestions (when they're asked for!). And, of course, you can all snack together when the creative part's done.

3. **You can support each other's work.** All the Girlz go to Reni's violin recitals and Suzy's soccer games. They all read the mounds of stuff Lily writes. They wouldn't miss a chance to rave about Kresha's artwork. And they're always bringing Zooey their moms' old decorating magazines because they know she's wild about changing her room around and giving it a new look every other week. We need our friends to help us keep going, especially when a little brother or well-meaning adult has just made a remark about our creative work that cuts us to the bone and we suddenly feel like giving the whole thing up and vegging in front of the TV.

4. **You can pray for each other.** Even fun stuff needs prayer!

Can you think of some friends you could "partner" with in play? Here are some direction-pointers. You don't have to fill them all in—just the ones that give you ideas right now. The rest may come later.

Do you have a cool creative idea, but it would take more than one person to pull it off? Think about all the people you know and pick, say, three (or more if you want) who would really be good at what you have in mind. Don't worry about whether they are currently your best friends (although they can be). Just write 'em down. It's the first step to making it happen!

Do you have several friends or even just girls you know a little bit who all seem interested in being creative like you are? Who are they?

Is there a place and a time where you could all get together and each do your own thing and then share a snack?

Where: _____

When: _____

Name your three very best friends.

_____

_____

_____

List one way you could support your friends' creativity (go to a friend's dance recital, loan that art easel you never use to a friend, or work the crossword puzzles a friend makes up).

_____

_____

_____

_____

Who are some people you would like to have pray for your creative efforts?

_____

_____

_____

_____

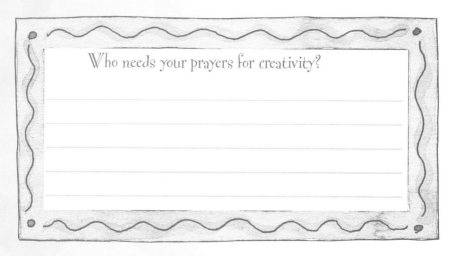

Who needs your prayers for creativity?

Now go back to the boxes and see if you can put any of those things into action. Don't try to do them all this week (or today!), but let them happen slowly. And be sure to listen to the ideas your partners in play are sure to have as things start to come together.

Girlz WANT TO KNOW

By now you probably have about a bajillion questions about "cooperative creating." So did the Girlz.

✿ *LILY: I love to do creative stuff with other people, but even the Girlz sometimes say I'm too bossy when I get going on something, or that the things I come up with are too elaborate and nobody could do them unless they were in Hollywood or something. It's so frustrating!*

Lily, Lily, Lily. You have this incredible creative mind and a ton of energy for using it. That's awesome. However, when you decide to partner up with people, you have to share the "idea-forming process" as well as the work! It's a pretty sure thing that when you always want to be in charge, your friends get resentful. Who wants to be part of something when they don't have any say-so in it?

If you let your friends offer their ideas and give someone else a chance to take some leadership once in a while, they probably won't think that what you all come up with together is too elaborate. It's the resentment that leads to the criticism.

Try putting your first idea out there and then not saying another word until each of the others has had her say. Don't argue with anyone's ideas before they've all been given. Even then, keep listening to hear what other people's objections might be to the various ideas. You may not always have to be the one who says, "I don't think that's gonna work" or "This is the best idea ever!"

It will take some self-control on your part, but God's there to help you. You might confide in your best friend to give you a signal when you're speaking out of turn (she tugs her ear—or she tugs your ear!).

❁ *KRESHA: Zooey is my best friend, but she's kind of a couch potato. When she comes over to my house and I suggest, "Let's make up some new jump-rope rhymes" or "I learned how to make ice shapes with cookie cutters—you want to make some with me?" she always says, "No—let's just watch TV" or "I wish you had a computer so we could play some games." Do you think she's just not creative?*

Everybody's creative! She just needs a little nudge—but don't try to force her. Why not try this? Next time you invite her over, have something already planned and tell her it's a surprise just for her. Set everything up so it's all ready to go—the flowerpots you're going to paint, the cupcakes you're going to decorate, or the beads you're going to string. Make the area where you're going to do your creative activity look really inviting—be creative! Don't worry about it being cheesy—go ahead and put up a sign that says, "Welcome to Kresha's KupCake Land!"

Then plunge right in with enthusiasm. If she whines, tell her there's a special snack when you're done, or tell her you'll do whatever she plans next time you go to her house. Chances are, she'll get into it, especially if you keep telling her you planned this just for her. And you are doing it for her. You're trying to help her feel that creative spark inside because, without it, you already know she's missing out on a lot. You don't have to tell her that. It can be a little secret between you and God!

✿ *RENI: In the summers, I go to visit my cousin for a couple of weeks, and she's creative like me. But she's such a know-it-all. If I say let's do something this way, she says that's not the way they do it at her school. If I want to choose one thing, she says nobody likes that, and we have to choose something else. And if I try to tell her about something I've done, like what I'm learning on the violin, she goes into this big long speech about how there's a girl at her school who's better than anybody on the violin and is going to some big private music school next year—blah, blah, blah. I don't need to be the best all the time or have everything go my way, but sometimes I get sick of her. Is that wrong?*

The feeling of being totally irritated by a know-it-all isn't bad in itself. In fact, it's pretty natural! The Pharisees, who were the biggest know-it-alls of all time, annoyed even Jesus. What you do with that feeling is all that matters.

If you say to your cousin, "Would you just shut up, you little windbag? I'm sick of you!" that would be, uh, wrong. That's hurtful and wouldn't solve anything. She probably would then go on to tell you that people "at her school" don't call each other names.

You could try just not talking about your own creative stuff so that she has nothing to go off on, but that's not really fair to you. Relationships are supposed to be for equal sharing.

Probably the best thing to do is ask her if she realizes what she's doing. You'd do it gently, of course, and maybe even with some humor—"Jennifer, do you realize that every time I bring up a subject, you know more about it than anybody on the planet?"

You might also want to avoid doing creative projects with her this summer, at least until she matures a little. Go to the movies, play board games, or ride bikes instead. Not everyone is the perfect partner in play for everyone else!

✿ *ZOOEY: I have this problem of being jealous of how creative all my friends are. Instead of being happy for Lily because she gets to be in a play or excited for Kresha because she's so good at drawing, I sometimes just want to smack them because I feel like such a moron next to them. I don't, of course, but sometimes I do slip and say something like, "Lily's a good actress, but she thinks she's "it" now." I don't really think that, but it kind of makes me feel better for a couple of minutes.*

For a couple of minutes—and then you feel worse than ever, right? Maybe it would help if you knew what causes that kind of jealousy in you. It's like a mask that you wear to cover up your fear. You probably would like to be in a play or try your hand at drawing cartoons or some of the other things the Girlz do, but you're afraid you won't be as good at it as Lily or Kresha.

That's when you have to look around you. God didn't create just one person who is good at drawing and one who is good at acting and one who can garden like a mad dog. God made tons of each, and there's room enough for the creative work of every single one of them. Instead of concentrating on feeling bad because everyone else has found her "thing," focus on finding yours!

Use this book to help you. Keep a little notepad with you, and whenever you think of, see, hear about, or read something that sounds like it would be fun to do, write it down. Don't start telling yourself that you'll never be able to do it—just write it down. When you have a list, pick one and think how you can dabble in it, like we did in chapter 4. Just do it for fun. Don't tell the other Girlz at first if you don't feel comfortable. Just do it for the joy of it, not for the finished product or for the way it makes you feel next to the Girlz. It will also help you to pray—for them! It's almost impossible to continue to feel jealous of someone's creativity when you're praying for them to have more.

Talking to God About It

Make a list of all the friends you have who are doing creative things—and remember that creativity isn't just about drawing, writing, or painting. It's about doing the things that express your sense of fun and delight. Next to each one, write down what you'd like to talk to God about on behalf of your friend. Lily, for example, prayed that Reni would continue to love playing the violin and not get too wrapped up in the competition. And she prayed that Zooey would have enough God-confidence to believe that she has creativity in her. Got the (creative) idea?

If I could change one thing about myself that would make me a better play partner, it would be . . .

What Do You Need?

**Whatever you ask for in prayer, believe
that you have received it, and it will be yours.**
Mark 11:24

Feeling pretty good about your sweet creative self, girl? You go!

As you continue to let yourself create, play, and take more delight in the things you do, you will continue to be happier—because you're making God happy. What a cool thing for God to see you using the gifts God supplied for you!

But as you go along, you'll probably feel the need for some other "supplies."

Lily was going like gangbusters (as only Lily can!), learning about acting by "dabbling." She read books about actors, studied the performances in the movies she rented, and did plays with the Girlz in Zooey's basement. But after a while, she decided she needed an *opportunity* to put her skills to work on a real stage.

Suzy checked a book out of the library on calligraphy and pretty quickly picked up the art of doing cool writing. But some of the really complex stuff was tough to do alone. She felt she needed some *lessons*.

Kresha found out by playing around with pencils and crayons that she really loved to draw. But she saw that there was only so far she could go with those basic supplies. She definitely needed some *tools* for creating art.

Reni loved practicing her violin and taking lessons. She enjoyed her violin the way most kids love an unexpected day off from school. But she was so into it she couldn't always tell if she was really getting better at it. She needed some *landmarks*.

Zooey finally found her "thing" in decorating rooms, and that helped her see that she had a knack for sewing, an eye for how things go together, and the ability to make something very cute out of what everyone else considered candidates for the trash pile. But Zooey's mom often smiled at Zooey's efforts as if to say, "Isn't that cute?" And when Zooey asked if she could get a subscription to a decorating magazine for her birthday, her mom said, "Aren't you getting a little carried away with this, Zooey?" What Zooey needed was some *respect* for her art from people like her mom.

It's natural when you get involved in what you love to do to realize there are things you need in order to enjoy it more fully and maybe even get better at it (which is part of the fun). Yet in all the previous chapters we've talked about using what you have and not spending a lot of money. How does that work then?

Let's start by making sure those "needs" are the real thing.

HOW IS THIS A **God Thing?**

As a God-loving person, you might be asking yourself: "Isn't it selfish to ask for things just so I can *play*?"

Not necessarily. Jesus himself taught the disciples to pray about everything. "Therefore I tell you, whatever you ask for in prayer, believe that you have received it, and it will be yours" (Mark 11:24).

That means, pray about anything that touches your life or the lives of others in an important way, and if you haven't figured out that creativity touches your life—go back to chapter 1!

Jesus did include one "catch." He said, "Have faith in God" (Mark 11:22). It's those people who love God and trust in him who get to ask for "everything." How do you know you're living a God-life?

- You worship God.
- You have a community of fellow God worshippers.
- You pray in your quiet place.
- You read about God in the Bible.
- You think about what God wants you to do, what Jesus would do in your situation, before you make a decision.
- You love other people the same way you love yourself—maybe even more!
- You think about God more and more all the time.
- You try to live the way Jesus did.

If you're doing all of that—or at least giving it your best shot—you are embracing the God-life and God will listen as you ask for what you need. It would only be selfish if:

- You ask for more than you need.
- You expect to always get what you want no matter what your other family members' needs are.
- You figure somebody should make a sacrifice to get you what you need.
- You know you might flit on to something else soon and waste what was given to you.
- You give God a deadline.
- You think you deserve it in a big way.

If you're "making art" as a way to use the gifts God has given you and to enjoy the God-life, it's all right to ask for what you need in order to do it. Jesus assures us of that in Luke 11:9:

- Ask and it will be given to you;
- seek and you will find;
- knock and the door will be opened to you.

CHECK Yourself OUT

Let's look at your own personal brand of creativity and see if there aren't some "supplies" you need. Then in the next section, we'll talk about how to get them.

Write down all the creative things you are now involved in or hope to be soon:

Now answer these questions about your creative activities:

Do you need *lessons* for any of those activities (guitar lessons, a tennis coach, an art class)? What kind? Do you know somebody who's a good teacher? Make a list.

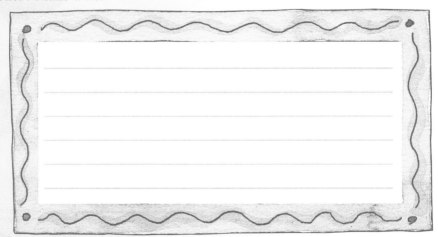

Do you need any *tools or supplies* (paints, brushes, notebooks, old magazines, an apron)? Make a dream list.

Do you need *opportunities* to practice your creative thing (a play to be in, a choir to sing in, an art gallery to visit, a beach where you can build mammoth sand castles)? What are they? Do you know of any coming up? List them.

Do you need things like understanding, privacy, or respect from other people when it comes to your creative craft (less teasing from your sister, Mom to let you hang your collages on your bedroom wall, Dad to take the time to read your newest poems)? List those.

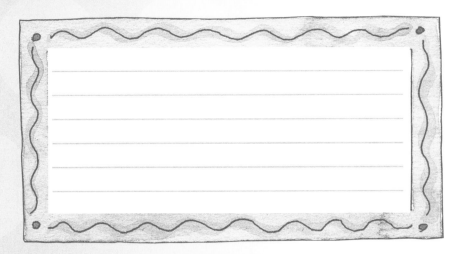

Do you need landmarks to let you know you're becoming more creative (when you've filled up a whole scrapbook, when your friends do the cheer you've made up, when your little sister sits still through the entire reading of the children's story you wrote and illustrated)? What things would let you know you're growing as a creative person?

Girlz WANT TO KNOW

✿ *LILY: So what do I do now—go to my parents with a list of stuff I need for the play the Girlz and I are going to put on, the drama workshop I want to go to this summer, and the three craft projects I have going? That's gonna go over big! I'll be the laughing stock of the living room!*

No, that doesn't sound like the best plan. What you need to do is this:

- Put the lessons, tools, opportunities, and so forth that you have on your list in order of their importance to you. That's called *prioritizing*.
- Now take the most important one and decide whether it's realistic to ask your parents for that. If it's a ten-dollar set of watercolors, that might be doable. If it's a trip to New York City to try out for *Annie,* you might need to rethink it!

- Think up some creative ways that you can help pay for or manage the thing you're asking for. Make a list of extra chores you could do around the house to earn the money for the workshop you want to go to. Offer to do the calling to find out the workshop details. Be ready with a plan for transportation to and from (maybe you've already bartered with your brother—he'll drive if you'll do his kitchen chores). In other words, be ready to show your parents that you are responsible enough to handle whatever it is you're asking for, that it's important to you, and that you'll make the necessary sacrifices.

- Timing is everything, so pick a time when your folks are not racing around looking for their keys or trying to fill out their tax forms. Asking at a bad time guarantees a flat "no."
- Be prepared to compromise. If they want to make some adjustments to your game plan, don't argue. After all, they're willing to work something out. A little is definitely better than nothing at all.
- No whining, foot-stomping, door-slamming, or eye-rolling allowed!

❁ *RENI: I don't understand the landmarks thing. Could you go over that again?*

Sure. Landmarks are simply events that let you know you're making progress as a creative person, just the way landmarks along the road let you know how much farther you need to go to get to your destination. You know, there's the big red barn—we're halfway to Grandma's; there's that Chinese restaurant—we have two miles to go. Since you want to get better and better and have more and more fun playing the violin, landmarks for you might be:

- Your parents get you a private teacher.
- You get into the school orchestra.
- You make first chair.
- You get to play a solo in a school orchestra concert.
- You're chosen for All-State Orchestra.

In something you do totally for fun, like designing cool evening gowns, landmarks you create might be:

- You finish ten drawings.
- The Girlz get excited about them.
- You get the nerve to show your work to your grandmother, who is a professional seamstress.

Sometimes landmarks are already there, as in your violin-playing list above. Sometimes you have to decide for yourself what they are, as in your evening gown list. And sometimes they'll just show up. What if, for example, you do show your designs to your grandmother, and she is so impressed she offers to teach you how to sew so you can make mini-gowns from your drawings and put them on dolls? That's an unexpected landmark. Enjoy keeping track of your landmarks in your journal.

✿ *SUZY: How do you find out about opportunities? I want to learn how to take better pictures.*

There are several ways you can find out what opportunities are out there for you to practice or improve your creative interest.

- Always keep your eyes and ears open. It's interesting how when you start looking for something, examples of it show up in places where you've never noticed it before. Must be a God thing.
- Ask people you know who are into that same thing, adults as well as kids. Is there someone at church parties and dinners who always has a camera hanging from a neck strap? Why not ask if that person knows about any photography classes for kids? Senior citizens are often the most helpful because they usually have more time than busy, working parents.
- Look for posters and fliers at camera shops or the film-processing center where you take your film (like Wal-Mart or K-mart). Ask the person behind the counter (or ask your mom to do it if you're too shy).
- Ask the art teacher at your school. Lots of visual artists also dabble in photography. If there are several of you who ask together, your teacher may decide to set up a photography workshop.
- Pray. Remember that we're supposed to ask for everything, large or small. You will *not* be wasting God's time!

✿ *ZOOEY: Kresha and I have the same problem—brothers! They're always getting into our stuff. Like my older brother used the glow-in-the-dark stars I had saved to put on my ceiling for his science project! And Kresha's little brother lost all the caps off her markers that I gave her for her birthday, and now they're all dried up and she can't use them. Our moms say stuff like, "Oh, for heaven's sake, it's just a couple of stars. I'd hate to see what you'd do over something really big." It's just—wrong!*

You really sound frustrated, and that's easy to understand. Other people—especially siblings who see you as just a sister rather than a creative human being—don't always get it. Here are a few suggestions for handling family members who think what's yours is theirs:

- Talk to your mom or dad about what things you own that you'd rather not share, especially if you've bought them with your own money. It would be to your advantage to also discuss the things you *are* willing to let other people use—as long as they ask.
- Keep the "no-share" creative tools out of sight (in the no-sharing zone) so nobody's tempted. Make a special box for your stuff and stash it in the back of your closet or under your bed.
- Let your siblings know *before* they discover your latest artistic purchase that it's off limits. Sometimes people really don't think you'll mind.
- Avoid screaming fits, pillow-throwing rages, and sisterly name-calling! Those don't work, and they won't do much to get your parents' support either.
- Consider asking your parents to get your brothers their own supplies if they're that fascinated by them—or when the next birthday or Christmas rolls around, give your brother a set of markers or a package of glow-in-the-dark stars as a gift.
- When you get the urge to throttle your brother for ripping you off, pray for wisdom—and self-control!

Just Do It

It's time to create your own game plan for that first new thing you need in order to continue making art and having a blast while doing it.

Look at the lists you made under **Check Yourself Out** earlier in this chapter. Pick out the one lesson, tool or supply, opportunity, positive attitude from others, or landmark that is the most important to you right now. If you couldn't have anything else but that one thing, what would it be?

Check the category it falls into:

_____ Lessons

_____ Tools/Supplies

_____ Opportunities

_____ Respect/Privacy/Understanding

_____ Landmarks

- If you circled *Lessons,* follow the advice we gave **Lily** and **Suzy** under **Girlz Want to Know**.
- If you circled *Tools/Supplies,* follow the advice we gave **Lily**.
- If you circled *Opportunities,* follow the advice we gave **Suzy**.
- If you circled *Respect/Privacy/Understanding,* follow the advice we gave **Zooey** and **Kresha**.
- If you circled *Landmarks,* follow the advice we gave **Reni**.

No matter which category you checked or game plan you follow to get what you need, in the process, pray, pray, pray. And did we mention pray? In fact, let's do some of that right now.

Talking to God About It

Write a heartfelt letter to God. Let it sound like you. In your letter, try to include these things (and others if you think of them):

❀ How you feel about God's creation.

❀ How you want to serve God through your own creativity.

❀ How you want to serve other people through your creativity.

❀ What you need from God in order to continue to be your best creative self.

❀ Thanksgiving for all God has already done for you that allows you to be creative.

❀ Confession of the things you've done with your creativity that might not be so wonderful—like telling your sister you're better at ballet than she is, that kind of thing.

Make sure that God will know from your letter that your creativity is fun and rich and delightful—but that it's all for him. Read it out loud to him. He's gonna love it!

Here's my wish list to make my next creative project an absolute dream . . .

A Thought to Go On

As you go off on your creative journey, tuck this thought into the back of your mind. You might not "get it" right now, but hold onto it anyway. That thought is:

As you continue to follow God's lead in your creativity, your whole life will become a work of art.

Your creative journey won't be just about the pictures you paint, the songs you write, or the houses you decorate. It will be about the life that inspires other people to serve God in the fun, delightful, zany, fresh way that you do.

So you go, girl! God loves you!

Lights, Action, Lily!

Nancy Rue

Zonder**kidz**

LILY

I hate having my picture taken," Reni said. "I always look so stupid."
"You do not either look stupid," Lily said.

"Yes, I do." Reni crossed her eyes to prove it, then shrugged. "It doesn't matter how I look in my school picture, though. My parents are having my portrait done at a studio so I can be holding my violin."

Their friend Suzy looked at Reni in awe. Lily did too. Reni was, after all, her best friend, and everything she did was amazing as far as Lily was concerned.

"I guess it doesn't matter about my picture," Suzy said, tilting her head so that her very dark, straight hair splashed across her cheek. "My soccer pictures are always better than my school pictures."

"That's nice for you two," Lily said. "But this is the only set I'm getting. And they have to be good. My dad's putting all our pictures on this family tree thing he's making for my grandmother for Christmas. He's got pictures of people on there from a hundred years ago. They all look like this."

Lily stood up straight and stiff and stared sternly into an imaginary camera lens. Suzy giggled softly.

"Okay, what's so funny? Let me in on the joke."

The three girls jumped — and then grinned — well, at least Reni and Lily did. Suzy ducked her head behind Lily's shoulder. It was Officer Horn, better known in kid circles as "Deputy Dog." She kept order around Cedar Hills Middle School with her mud-brown, piercing stare and her thumbs hooked into her belt. Although the Girlz — Lily, Reni, Suzy, Zooey, and Kresha — had had their run-ins with her at the beginning of the year, she was their "bud" now — as long as they played by the rules. Deputy Dog didn't cut any slack to those who didn't.

"Do that face for her, Lily," Reni said.

Lily was about to when there was a shriek from the front of the line, up close to where the photographer was snapping pictures. Deputy Dog's ears practically stood on end.

"Excuse me, ladies," she said, and strolled toward the front.

Lily stood on her tiptoes to check out the action.

"What's going on?" Reni asked.

Lily groaned. It was, of course, Ashley Adamson and her clone-friend Chelsea. Shad Shifferdecker was up there holding what appeared to be Ashley's picture order form over his head, and Ashley was jumping for it and missing — on purpose, from what Lily could tell. *That girl is so boy crazy,* Lily thought, *it makes me want to reach for a barf bag.*

"Is it Ashley?" Reni said.

"Who else?"

"And Shad?"

"Uh-huh."

"Are they still going out?" Suzy said.

Lily rolled her eyes. "That's what she says. Where do people 'go' when they say they're 'going out'? I know Ashley's parents don't let her date. She's twelve!"

"I don't know," Reni said. "They let her get away with everything. Did you see how short her skirt is?"

"She'll get in trouble for that with Deputy Dog," Suzy said. And then she tugged anxiously at her own skirt.

"Even if they do let her date," Lily said, "who would want to go out with Shad Shifferdecker anyway? Blech!"

"He's getting cuter," Reni said.

"Gross! He's sure not getting nicer!"

"Shh, Lily!" Suzy whispered. "Deputy Dog's looking back here!"

Lily lowered her voice, and Reni and Suzy leaned their heads in. "Friday, when I forgot my lunch," Lily said, "and I had to go through the food line, he was standing behind me, pretending like he was pulling bugs out of my hair—and eating them!"

"That is *so* disgusting!" Reni said.

"It's definitely not cute," Lily said. She gave her mane of curly red hair a toss. "As soon as I got home, I got out the shampoo. It was like I could feel his cooties crawling around on my scalp."

Suzy shivered. Reni scratched her own head between two of her African black-beaded braids.

"Here she comes!" Suzy said, and ducked behind Lily again.

It was Ashley, sauntering from the picture-taking area and glancing over her shoulder while giving her turned-up blonde hair a flip.

"Move along, Adamson," Deputy Dog called to her in a bored voice. "The fans are not clamoring for more. You're finished here."

"Hel-lo-o! I'm waiting for Sha-ad," Ashley said.

"You're waiting to get yourself busted with that tone," Deputy Dog said. "Now get back to class."

Ashley rolled her eyes, threw her hair back, and stalked away.

As the line shuffled forward, Lily felt someone at her elbow and looked around to see Chelsea beside her.

"Did you forget it was picture day, Robbins?" Chelsea asked.

Lily could already feel her teeth clenching together. "No," she said.

"Oh — so you meant for your hair to look like that." She put her hands up, several inches from each side of her head, and said, "Poof!"

"You got a problem with that?" Reni said.

"No," Chelsea said. She curled her lip, leaving a trail of lip gloss under her nose. "But Robbins obviously has one. Ashley's right — she's so — *weird.*"

Then she swung herself around and at a fast walk went after Ashley, who was loitering in the gym doorway. Chelsea's short vinyl skirt twitched back and forth as she went.

"You're not weird, Lily," Suzy said. "I think you're beautiful."

"Thanks," Lily said.

She composed herself and turned to move ahead with the line. She knew better than to pay attention to Ashley, Chelsea, Bernadette, and the rest of the "popular" kids. And she knew she wasn't weird. Granted, she had the thickest, reddest, curliest hair in the whole school — and she was tall — and she got really into the things she was jazzed about. But that didn't make her *weird.* It just made her — *unique.*

Of course, right now she wasn't feeling particularly special, not after hearing about Reni's picture with her violin and Suzy's with a soccer ball.

Lily was at that point again — the point where she didn't have anything going that was just hers — that made her stand out — and it was even more obvious at home. Her older brother Art was already being asked to apply at different music schools, and he was only a junior. Her little brother Joe had enough sports trophies in his room to start his own store, and he was only ten. Even her parents were getting more and more recognition. Mom was taking over as head of the athletic department at the high school while the real guy was having surgery, and Dad had just submitted a book that was probably going to get published.

And here I am again, Lily thought. *I'm generic. I'm like the potato chips that come in the white bag with the black print—blah, bland, cardboard—*

"Lily—the line's moving," Reni said behind her.

Lily lurched forward into the space that had been left between her and Marcie McCleary. Marcie didn't seem to notice. She was too busy adjusting all the chains that were hanging from her jacket, from her arms, and out of the pockets of her too-big jeans.

Reni poked Lily and pointed to Marcie, her face a question mark. Lily knew what she meant, and she had the same question: *What is happening to Marcie? She's turning into a gang chick or something.*

Marcie's chain obsession also caught Deputy Dog's eye. "McCleary—come here—I want to talk to you," she said.

Marcie scurried over to her. Ahead, Shad was just taking his seat in front of the camera, and he was taking full advantage of Deputy Dog's turned-away head. Lily watched as he slouched on the stool, parked his arms on his thighs, and gave the photographer a "Whasup?" look. His snappy little eyes sparkled in the lights and for once didn't look so close together.

"Hey," Reni whispered, "he got his braces off. I told you he was getting cuter."

"Sit up, son," the photographer said.

Shad did—so straight he looked like he had a pole for a spine. Several kids ahead of Lily laughed appreciatively. Lily didn't.

"Not that straight," the photographer said. "Come on, give me something natural."

Shad grinned a half-grin, eyebrows arched up to the swish of hair that wasn't shaved. The photographer snapped the camera, and the kids in the front of the line clapped.

"That's gonna be *so* good!" some girl said.

"Oh, brother," Lily said.

There were only two people ahead of Lily now, and with Deputy Dog still preoccupied with Marcie and her chains, Shad shoved his hands into the pockets of his jeans, yanked them down below his boxers, and began to work the line. Lily folded her arms and turned her back in his direction.

That didn't keep Shad from stopping behind her. She could feel him investigating her curls.

"Touch it and you'll draw back a nub," Lily said.

"Ooh—I'm scared. I'm terrified," Shad said.

"Give it up, Shifferdecker," Reni said. "Move up, Lily—you're gonna be next."

Lily edged sideways so she didn't have to turn around and look at Shad. For all she knew, he had given up and left. She should be so lucky.

"I'm gonna wait and see how that hair looks under them lights," Shad said. "Wait—let me get my sunglasses out."

Lily ignored him and slid onto the stool. The photographer peered at her over the camera and said, "Smile, honey."

Lily did. Ever since last year when she'd gone to modeling school, she hadn't minded having her picture taken. But having Shad there definitely made it hard to concentrate.

"Help—help—I'm blind!" Shad said. "She blinded me!"

Crawl back into the hole you came out of, Lily thought. But she didn't just think it. She knew she looked it, too, as she shot Shad a disdainful glare. The photographer chose that moment to snap the picture. Behind him, Reni and Suzy looked horrified.

"Next, please," the photographer said.

"But I wasn't ready!" Lily said. "I was looking over there and doing this!" She reenacted the face. By now, the kids behind Suzy and Reni were craning their necks like Gumby dolls and snickering.

"Can't you take it over?" Lily said.

"Nope," the photographer said. "Wait 'til these come out, and if you don't like them, you can come back for retakes."

"When's that gonna be?" Lily said.

"Middle of December."

"But — "

"Next, please?"

As Lily walked out of the light, she could feel the hot blotches on her face. That always happened when she got mad — and right now, she was surprised there wasn't steam coming out of her ears too. She stomped after Shad with her fists doubled, but he was nowhere in sight outside the gym. It figured. He'd seen Lily's temper in action before.

Lily, her mind reeling, stopped in the hallway and looked around. She had to get to class, but later — later, he was *so* gonna get it from her. She marched out of the gym wing and up the stairs toward Mrs. Reinhold's room, where a detention would be waiting if she didn't get there in what Mrs. R. called "a timely fashion."

Shad wasn't in that class — it was accelerated English, and Shad wasn't much of a student. Maybe that was a good thing, since strict Mrs. Reinhold (Mrs. Stranglehold, Ashley and her friends called her behind her back) wouldn't give Lily a chance to get back at him under her hawk eyes.

Lily was fuming about that as she rounded the corner and spotted Shad standing in the middle of the hall. He was obviously mimicking Lily's signature glare for his two friends — Daniel and Leo.

Lily clenched her fists and stomped up behind him. Leo and Daniel slunk off like a pair of weasels as Shad turned around to face Lily and began an evil grin that drew his beady little eyes close together over his nose.

"You are an absurd little creep," Lily said.

"Cool," Shad said.

"No, it is *not* cool. It is *so* not cool. That picture is going on a family heirloom, not that you care."

"Not that I even know what an air-loom is," Shad said. "It's goin' on the side of a plane? Cool—"

"No, moron! Forget it. But you are *so* paying for it if I have to have retakes."

"I ain't payin' for the camera—which you broke when you looked in it."

Lily narrowed her eyes at him and showed her teeth—kind of the way her dog Otto did when she made him drop a pen of hers he was chewing. Shad made the same face back—only uglier.

"You are so immature," she said. "My *dog* is more grown up than you are."

"Yeah?" Shad said. His eyes sparkled. "Well, *my* dog is better *lookin'* than you are. Come to think of it, my little sister's pet guinea pig is better lookin' than you are."

Lily maintained her narrow-eyed stare. "Anybody else?" she said.

"Nah—that's all the pets we got."

"I believe round one goes to the young man," said a voice from the doorway.

Lily froze. It was Mrs. Reinhold.

Chapter 2

*T*hat's it, Lily thought. My life is over. I might as well just lie down right here in the hall and die.

It didn't even help that Reni and Suzy appeared around the corner just then. There was no comfort when you were up against Mrs. Reinhold.

Lily turned to look at her, just as Mrs. Reinhold was motioning for Reni and Suzy to go on into the classroom. Then she stood over Lily and Shad and adjusted her teeny-weeny glasses. Shad looked at his feet, clad in Doc Martens, the smirk still on his face.

"Interesting little dialogue," Mrs. Reinhold said.

Lily opened her mouth to explain, but Mrs. Reinhold put up her hand.

"You," she said to Shad. "Where do you belong?"

Shad mumbled something out of the side of his mouth and continued to smirk at his shoes.

"Then go there," Mrs. Reinhold said.

Shad shrugged, shoved his hands into his pockets, and ambled off as if he were going window-shopping.

"I'm sorry if we were too loud," Lily said. "But he — "

Again, Mrs. Reinhold put her hand up. "I would like for you to meet me back here during lunch," she said. "Did you bring a sack lunch today?"

Lily could only nod.

"Good — bring that with you and we'll eat here."

"Okay," Lily said. She could feel her face wanting to crumple, and she willed herself not to cry until she was at least in her seat, behind a book or something.

"This is not a punishment, Lilianna," Mrs. Reinhold said. "There is just something I would like to speak with you about. Now — what was that young man's name that you were out here sparring with?"

That Lily was glad to tell her. If Shad had gotten off scot-free, she would have been beyond mad.

Mrs. Reinhold seemed to be locking the information into her memory as she nodded. "All right," she said. "Go on inside. The assignment is on the board."

Lily nodded and went for the door, but she stopped halfway there and looked back at Mrs. Reinhold. "I'm sorry. I really am. When we were — "

"Please, Lilianna," Mrs. Reinhold said. "You are such an obsessive child."

Lily didn't know what "obsessive" meant, but she was sure it couldn't be good. When she got to her desk, behind Ashley, she sank heavily into the seat.

"Busted," Ashley whispered over her shoulder.

Lily ignored her, although she would rather have Ashley hiss insults at her all day than be in trouble with Mrs. Reinhold. She had worked so hard to get her approval.

After class, Lily was answering Suzy and Reni's barrage of questions on the way to geography when they ran into Zooey and Kresha.

"Zooey — you look so cute!" Suzy said.

It was true. There was a time when Zooey had been the plump one in the group, but ever since the beginning of the school year, she'd been losing what she called her "baby fat." That meant having to get new clothes, and Zooey was decked out in them now. She looked like an ad for the Gap.

Zooey beamed and did a twirl so they could all take in the khaki jumper. All, that is, except for Kresha, who was frowning at her picture order form.

"What's wrong?" Lily said.

"I can no understand dis," Kresha said. "What this means — g-e-n-d-e-r?" She scowled at Lily from beneath her sandy-brown bangs.

"That means whether you're a boy or a girl," Lily said.

Kresha looked at the form and frowned again. "This say M or F."

"Male or female."

"Oh," Kresha said. Her smile lit up her face and then faded again. "What I am?" she said.

Zooey slapped her hand over her mouth to keep from giggling, but Suzy poked her in the side anyway. They were all careful not to hurt Kresha's feelings. She was Croatian, and although she was doing well with her English, it was still a struggle for her sometimes.

"You're female," Lily told her. "Boys are male. Boys are also idiots, and I can't stand them."

"Oh," Kresha said. She squinted at the form. "That is on here?"

"No — Lily's just venting," Reni said.

"What happened?" Zooey said, her big eyes wide.

"She can tell you at lunch," Suzy said, glancing nervously at her watch.

"I won't be at lunch," Lily said. "Mrs. Reinhold wants to see me."

The four faces in front of her looked stricken.

"Yeah," Lily said. "I know."

Fourth-period geography class usually dragged because their young teacher Ms. Ferringer was so unorganized, but that day it went by all too quickly. When the bell rang, Lily felt her stomach tying itself into knots.

Reni passed her a Girlz-Gram before she rushed off to the orchestra room for practice, and Lily read it as she dragged herself to Mrs. Reinhold's room.

You were right. Shad was wrong. Tell Mrs. R. It'll be okay.
— Reni

Although it was written in the Girlz usual telegram style, it did make Lily feel a little better as she pulled open the door to Mrs. R.'s room. Lily was always good at explaining things. Maybe it *would* be okay.

She was a little stunned, however, when she walked into the room and saw six other people there.

Wow, Lily thought. *Mrs. Reinhold must have radar or something to get this many people for lunch detention.*

It was odd, though, because she recognized most of the kids as being eighth graders, and Mrs. Reinhold taught mostly seventh grade except for the accelerated eighth-grade English class. These weren't the kind of kids that usually got into trouble.

Lily grunted to herself. *I'm not either!* she thought. *From now on, I'm never going to speak to Shad Shifferdecker again. I'm going to pretend he doesn't exist.*

She was counting up the number of times she had made that vow to herself when Mrs. Reinhold said, "All right, people, listen up. Is everyone here?"

It wasn't actually a question you answered, although one rather chubby eighth-grade boy did raise his hand and say, "I am!"

"Thank you, Philip," Mrs. Reinhold said dryly. She counted kids with her finger and frowned. "I'm missing one."

"No, you're not," Phillip said, pointing to the door.

Shad was just sauntering in. Lily turned her head sharply so she wouldn't have to look at him.

"Good. I'll get started," Mrs. Reinhold said. "Listen carefully to what I'm about to tell you because I only have time to explain it once. As you will see, time is of the essence. If when I am finished you decide that you do not want to participate in the program, you may opt to leave at that time."

Lily hoped she didn't look as confused as she felt. This was a weird kind of detention—

"Now, then," Mrs. Reinhold said. "I have chosen promising students from my classes—as well as one I selected off the street."

She gave Shad a pointed look, and to Lily's disgust he raised a fist as if he'd just won an Olympic gold medal.

"I am asking you," Mrs. Reinhold went on, "to participate in a pilot program that is being done district-wide to encourage students to study Shakespeare."

"What's that?" Shad asked.

She gave him a Reinhold glare. He slumped down in the seat. Lily rolled her eyes.

"Shakespeare, as most of you know, was a great Renaissance playwright who left us some of the richest, most enduring plays in the English language."

Shad pretended to snore. If Mrs. Reinhold heard him, she didn't let on.

"Each participating school is to choose a group of students who will put together scenes from a Shakespearean play and perform them at a festival on November 20."

"Do we get out of school to go to this thing?" said a boy with a ponytail that cascaded down from a partially shaved head.

"No — it's a Saturday, Wesley," Mrs. Reinhold said.

Shad bolted up in his seat. "A Saturday?" he said.

"You will note that the date is only three weeks away," Mrs. Reinhold went on. "I received the word late, and that is why I have handpicked students myself rather than holding auditions."

"I gotta do school stuff on a Saturday?" Shad said.

"I know most of you well enough to see that you are bright, capable, creative — "

"I ain't workin' on no Saturday — "

" — and have some natural acting ability."

Mrs. Reinhold looked at Shad, who stopped in the middle of another protest against working weekends and let half a grin appear.

"Acting ability?" he said.

"Yes," Mrs. Reinhold said.

She left Shad puzzling over that and continued. "I have already cast the roles, and I have your scripts ready. If you are going to participate in this program, you will be expected to be here during lunch every day between now and the twentieth. You will be expected to learn lines and take direction from college theater students who are coming in to assist us."

"This sounds hard," said a girl with glasses and a slightly off-center ponytail.

"It is definitely challenging," Mrs. Reinhold said.

"I'm outta here then," Shad said.

"The college students are coming in to teach you how to do stage combat choreography. To use the vernacular, you will learn how to throw each other around on stage."

Shad stopped halfway out of his desk and grinned again. "You mean, like fights and stuff?" he said.

"Yes," Mrs. Reinhold said.

Shad said, "All right!"

Next to him a kid with a completely shaved head held up his hand for Shad to give him a high five.

"Gary, Shad," Mrs. Reinhold said, "if you have finished the formalities."

Gary grinned. Shad looked baffled.

Oh, brother, Lily thought with an inner groan. *Shad doesn't even know what formalities are. He oughta be just great at Shakespeare.*

She'd never actually read any of Shakespeare's plays herself, but she'd heard Dad talk about them—he was an English professor, after all—and she knew they had a lot of hard words and fancy language. It *would* be a challenge—for Lily. For Shad, she was sure it would be impossible.

"Our scenes will be taken from *The Taming of the Shrew,*" Mrs. Reinhold said, "which is one of Shakespeare's comedies. We will be doing three scenes."

She picked up several sets of papers from her desk, and everyone in the room sat up straighter in their seats—except for Shad, who played a soft rendition of "Wipe Out" on the desktop with his fingers. But he was watching Mrs. Reinhold intently.

"Before I hand these out," she said, "let me ask if there is anyone who would rather not participate in this program. There will be no penalty for excusing yourself—I know Shakespeare is not for everyone—but my firsthand knowledge of each of you indicates to me that you are all up to this challenge."

Lily stared at her. How did Mrs. Reinhold know anything about Shad? Until a few hours ago, she didn't even know his name.

"Now then," Mrs. Reinhold said, "this first scene is for four males—but because we have a plethora of girls, I am asking two of you young ladies to play the parts of old men. You will be costumed complete with mustaches, beards, whatever it takes to transform you."

I don't really want to play an old man, Lily thought. She was already envisioning herself at center stage in a gorgeous Renaissance gown dripping with gold braid. She held her breath.

"Fiona," Mrs. R. said to an African-American girl who was even skinnier than Kresha, "would you and Natalie take these crossover parts?"

Fiona didn't look any too pleased, and neither did Natalie, the girl with the glasses and the crooked ponytail. At least—they didn't until Mrs. Reinhold handed the next script to Gary, the kid with the ponytail. Reni would have said he was "cute." They also seemed to like Philip, the chubby kid, and the four of them shoved their desks together and began to whisper excitedly. Lily looked around. She didn't know Wesley or the other girl, a pretty, dimpled eighth-grader whose blonde hair was cut in a perfect bob. She wondered if either one of them would be very excited about working with her.

"Wesley, you and Hilary will work together as Bianca and Lucentio."

"Who are they?" Hilary said, taking the script as if it were a poisonous snake.

Lily didn't hear the answer. She was frozen to the seat. The only two people left were herself—and Shad.

"Ah—you two," Mrs. Reinhold said. It was rare to see her smile, but she was beaming broadly at Shad and Lily, as if she were enjoying some joke nobody else understood. Lily certainly didn't get it.

"Shad," she said, "you will play the part of Petruchio. Lilianna—you will be Katharina—better known as Kate."

"Are we in the same scene?" Lily said.

Mrs. Reinhold's eyebrows twisted. "Yes—unless you each want to do a monologue."

"What's a monologue?" Shad said.

"When you have a long piece to say by yourself," Mrs. Reinhold said.

"Forget that—no way." Shad took the script and then suddenly looked up. "Hey," he said. "I gotta do this with Snobbins?"

He jerked his head toward Lily.

"With Lilianna?" Mrs. Reinhold said. "Yes. And from what I saw out in the hall this morning, I think you two are perfectly matched for this scene."

Lily stared from her to the script and back again, until Mrs. Reinhold wandered over to one of the other groups. Lily looked at the writing in italics at the top of the scene.

Petruchio has come to convince Katharina to marry him.

Lily sagged all the way down in her seat.

Mrs. Reinhold had been wrong. This *was* a punishment.

Pick up a copy today at your local bookstore!

Softcover 0-310-70249-6

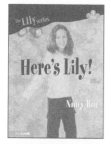

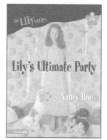
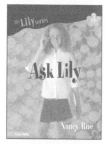

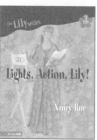

NIV Young Women of Faith Bible
GENERAL EDITOR SUSIE SHELLENBERGER

Designed just for girls ages 8-12, the *NIV Young Women of Faith Bible* not only has a trendy, cool look, it's packed with fun to read in-text features that spark interest, provide insight, highlight key foundational portions of Scripture, and more. Discover how to apply God's word to your everyday life with the *NIV Young Women of Faith Bible*.

Hardcover 0-310-91394-2
Softcover 0-310-70278-X
Slate Leather–Look™ 0-310-70485-5
Periwinkle Leather–Look™ 0-310-70486-3

Available now at your local bookstore!

Zonderkidz.

Now Available

Rough & Rugged Lily (Book 9)
Softcover 0-310-70260-7

The Year 'Round Holiday Book companion

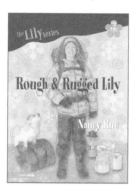

Lily Speaks! (Book 10)
Softcover 0-310-70262-3

The Values & Virtues Book companion

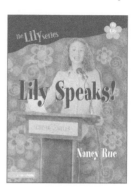

The Year 'Round Holiday Book ... It's a God Thing!
Softcover 0-310-70256-9

Rough & Rugged Lily companion

The Values & Virtues Book ... It's a God Thing!
Softcover 0-310-70257-7

Lily Speaks! companion

Zonder**kidz**.

We want to hear from you. Please send your comments about this
book to us in care of the address below. Thank you.

Zonderkidz™

Grand Rapids, MI 49530
www.zonderkidz.com